RED INK

A Guide to Understanding the Deficit Dilemma

by Harold A. Hovey
with Richard J. Dennis
Foreword by Allen Sinai

Roosevelt Center for American Policy Studies
316 Pennsylvania Avenue, S.E., Suite 500
Washington, DC 20003
250 South Wacker Drive, Suite 1250
Chicago, IL 60606

Copyright © 1985 by the Roosevelt Center for American Policy Studies
All rights reserved, including the right to reproduce this book or portions thereof in any form whatsoever.

ISBN: 0-913217-04-2
Library of Congress Catalog Card Number 85-61510

First Roosevelt Center Books printing May, 1985

Printed in the U.S.A.

BOARD OF TRUSTEES

The Roosevelt Center is a new kind of American institution. Its uniqueness is in its commitment to helping individual Americans reach independent judgments on critical national policy issues and then to take those judgments into the policy decision-making process.

The Center's basic technique is to develop and present a comprehensive range of reasoned policy options—a virtual policy multiple-choice test—supported by understandable background material and a growing array of techniques and mechanisms for simulating and supporting the process of coming to judgment. In every policy project, the Center's basic objective is to bring individual Americans confidently to the frontier of policy in order that they might make their own choices and seek to implement them within the American political system.

This book is a policy primer, one of the products which the Center produces for virtually all of its policy projects. Role-playing games, like the DEBTBUSTERS game described on the last page of this book, are also frequent Center products. This family of products also includes policy road maps, op-ed pieces, conference reports, and instructional and documentary films.

In all cases, the Center maintains a strictly nonpartisan posture. This decision to forego the more traditional institutional approach of advocating particular policy alternatives—or supporting individuals who themselves pursue such advocacy—was carefully made. It stems from a bedrock belief that the genius of American society springs from a free market in ideas, and that policy decision-making should be no exception.

TABLE OF CONTENTS

PREFACE

Welcome to the Roosevelt Center's handbook on the federal deficit.
The fact that you're reading this book probably means you are concerned about the deficit problem. We hope that this book will help you learn more about the origin of the deficit, its effects, and the alternatives for dealing with it.

We are committed to the idea that our country will work better if people understand the choices we make as a nation. That's our only purpose. We have some views about the dangers posed by large deficits and about the kinds of compromises that are needed to deal with the federal budget. But we are not proposing a specific deficit reduction target or plan, and we have tried to formulate a balanced presentation.

After you have read this book, you may find you have an opinion about how large a deficit, if any, the federal government should run and about what changes should be made in federal spending and tax policy to achieve your goal. At the end, we have a section suggesting how your opinion can make a difference—if you want it to.

Richard Dennis, Chairman
Roosevelt Center for American Policy Studies

Harold A. Hovey, Economist
Roosevelt Center for American Policy Studies

FOREWORD

This book is a primer on federal budget deficits and federal debt: their meaning, the amounts involved, impacts and effects, choices available on taxes and spending to reduce the deficits, and the budget-making process in Washington.

The federal budget deficit is the key issue of the day. The current string of unprecedented big deficits started in 1981—the result of a deep recession, massive tax cuts for individuals and business, and a shift in spending priorities that involved greater defense spending and intended cuts in nondefense spending that did not materialize. Large reductions of inflation rates also have worsened the deficits, since lower inflation automatically produced lower tax revenues until indexation began in 1985. A period of unprecedented high nominal interest rates also is a prime contributor to the huge deficits, with substantial increases for government net interest expense stemming from the deficits themselves, heavy Treasury financing, and central bank policies designed to prevent reinflation.

The Roosevelt Center's handbook brings the reader into the center of the budget debate, giving the facts and arguments one needs to be an informed participant in helping to resolve the deficit problem. The book is clearly and simply written, extraordinarily intuitive in its approach, and deals with one of the most difficult and complicated topics in economics in terms layperson can understand. How federal spending, taxing, and borrowing work to create deficits is explained at the outset. What magnitudes of deficits and debt are likely under current prospects are indicated. Pros and cons of the budget deficit are discussed, as well as its impact on interest rates, foreign trade, specific sectors of the economy, jobs and saving.

The authors then move on to deal with the various alternatives for reducing the federal budget deficit. The full range of options to reduce spending is shown, with the choices on defense spending, entitlements—means-tested and non-means-tested—and other types of nondefense outlays indicated and evaluated. Revenue alternatives are also examined, ranging from raising revenues through "new taxes," such as a value-added tax (VAT), a wealth or assets tax, oil or energy taxes, to "old" measures such as increased excise taxes or income tax surcharges. Reforming the current tax system by base-broadening is discussed as well. Estimates of potential additional revenues are presented for each option.

ix

Finally, the budget-making process itself is discussed, with a clear explanation of choices on procedures, such as a balanced budget amendment or line-item veto, that could hold the deficits down. The book also contains an innovative and creative feature— directions to the reader on how next to proceed. A section, "The Federal Budget Deficit: Do Something About It!" lays out, in game format (the DEBTBUSTER game), a framework for a detailed deficit reduction program designed by the reader. Additional readings, a simple worksheet for involving the reader in a plan to reduce the deficit, and a form letter with a suggested outline for writing to Congress are included.

The book lays out the problems and choices in an easily understandable format, illuminates and explains some very difficult ideas and concepts, and calls the reader to action. It is a valuable tool that will enable the public to participate in resolving the number one economic issue facing the nation— how to reduce the flow of red ink in the federal budget in an efficient and acceptable manner to help sustain growth and prosperity through the rest of this decade and beyond.

Allen Sinai
Chief Economist and Managing Director
  Shearson Lehman Brothers, Inc. and
  Adjunct Professor of Economics
  Graduate School of Business, New York University

Chapter One

A Disaster Scenario

Saturday, October 9, 2004

Congress Repudiates Debt

"Debt Burden Impossibly Large"
Maintains Sen. Spender

In a late-night session Friday, Congress finally passed a budget for fiscal year 2005, including an unexpected amendment to repudiate all government debt. If the budget is signed by the President as expected, it will be the first time in the country's history that the principal on any government debt has been repudiated, wiping out approximately $21 trillion of wealth in the United States and overseas.

Sen. Fred Spender, chairman of the committee on budget reform who was contacted late last night, said, "It was the only way to pass any kind of budget. The fact that it is already October shows the difficulty of the problem that we faced. With the budget passed, we will have a balanced budget, and we can rid this generation of the burdensome legacy left us by the insane policies of the 1980s and '90s." In response to further questions, Sen. Spender admitted the debt repudiation amounted to a one-time tax on the holders of government debt, but "with the debt burden so impossibly large, there was nothing else to do," he maintained. "For 2005 we projected interest payments of $2.2 trillion, generating a deficit of $2.4 trillion. This brings total government debt to $21 trillion in an economy whose GNP is $12.4 trillion. With a deficit of nearly 20% of GNP and a debt of 170% of GNP, we cannot function."

The text of the budget amendment was worked out in top-secret meetings of the committee on budget reform and included members of both Houses of Congress, officials of the Federal Reserve, the President's office, and attorneys from the Justice Department. No administration officials could be reached for comment, but the White House issued a statement saying that a televised press conference would be held at 8:00 p.m. EST today.

The government's action will start a week of financial market turmoil. Hundreds of corporations are expected to ask the New York Stock Exchange to suspend trading in their shares pending announcements by their respective boards of directors. Last week, the Dow Jones Industrial Average fell to its lowest in 37 years, ending the week at 500. Since more than one-quarter of the issues in the Dow were not trading, however, the index is highly inaccurate. How much lower prices will be on the next opening, no one can say.

Officers of many brokerage and investment banking houses have called for emergency work by their employees through this three-day weekend to analyze the impact of the repudiation on exchange-traded companies. "A very large number of companies keep all working capital in short-term government securities, mainly T-bills," said Gerald Bigbiz, the president of Boldman-Bachs. "They may all be in a very difficult situation on Tuesday." The New York Stock Exchange is considering staying closed on Tuesday after the Columbus Day holiday to allow more time for investors to "become aware of all the options open to them," a spokesman for the Exchange said.

Some companies have already shut down. "All of our working capital was in Treasury bills," said John Pilot, president of Unlimited Airlines. "We cannot pay employees or suppliers. We cannot pay airport fees. All flights are immediately canceled." (He estimates that thousands of people would be stranded at airports.) "There is nothing we can do," he added. Six of the major airlines are in the same position. George Action, president of Consolidated Technologies, has called for companies to use barter. "Unless we all agree to maintain business as usual, no company will survive." He has called for a conference of business and labor leaders tomorrow to work out a system of barter transactions which will be "beyond the power of government to destroy." Even if an agreement is reached before Tuesday, unemployment is expected to rise; however, no one will speculate how high it might go.

Even though all European markets have been closed since the budget passed, rumors of private transactions between major investors show that most assets have fallen precipitously as investors scurry to sell everything to raise cash for immediate needs. In its morning edition, the French newspaper *Le Monde* called the U.S. government action "the payoff of the greatest confidence game every perpetrated upon the human race. Borrow, borrow, borrow—then get out of town leaving no forwarding address. It is the coward's way out." The *London Times* said, "The worldwide impact will be devastating." The usually reserved Swiss rioted in front of the U.S. Embassy in Berne, breaking windows and burning U.S. government vehicles in the courtyards around the building.

John Hindsight, an economist for Absolutely Big Bank said, "It's easy to see now how we got into this mess. The last time that something simple could have been done was in the 1980s. If budget deficits had been dealt with then, we would not have come to this. But all the proposals were very timid, because actually running a balanced budget then was thought of as a drastic measure. If only they had known the future.

"In the middle 1980s, people convinced themselves that steady economic growth would eliminate the budget deficit problem even though they had huge deficits in 1984, a good growth year. Or they convinced themselves that deficits did not matter, since 1984 was so good in the face of deficits. In fact, we did have economic growth all through the 1980s and 1990s, and early 2000s, with no major recessions. We averaged 1% real growth since that golden year of 1984 and kept non-interest spending and tax rates about constant as a percentage of GNP, except that spending exploded because of the effect of interest compounding on the national debt. That explosion of debt kept real interest rates at the same level as 20 years ago, a level then thought unsustainable, but now seen as the market's rational response to deficits out of control. We were in a situation in which the status quo was the road to oblivion, but people simply denied what should have been obvious. We were in deep trouble then. The 'growth solution' became a part of the conventional wisdom which could not be challenged and the 'ostrich solution' was popular. Now we pay the piper.''

* * * * *

This scenario need not ever become a reality, and in all probability it won't. The assumptions underlying it are far more pessimistic than those generally accepted by economists and politicians. But the scenario does illustrate the nature of the problems we will face down the road if we fail to give the budget deficit our most serious attention. It is our hope that the material in the following chapters will help you clarify your own thinking and formulate your own approach to this urgent national problem.

As you think about this problem, keep in mind that it has roots not just in the behavior of government, but in the desires of the American people. Our society is divided into an enormous variety of groups. Many of them attach great significance to one or more categories of spending (e.g., defense, domestic social programs, social security). From their perspective, continuing these programs with a large deficit is less of an evil than slashing them to reduce the deficit. Their preferred alternative is typically some combination of tax increases and cuts in programs not of direct interest to them. A continuing risk is that practically all such groups will agree on the need to reduce deficits but that each group will be able to block avenues of deficit reduction adversely affecting it. Many people think that just this process has led to the recent deficit deadlock.

3

Chapter Two

Debts And Deficits

THE NATURE AND SIZE OF THE
FEDERAL DEFICIT AND DEBT

Practically every American understands being in debt. Most Americans use debt to make long-term capital investments such as homes and cars. Many also finance everyday consumption, such as vacations and clothing, with credit cards. They recognize that going into debt requires that interest be paid and that the principal must eventually be repaid as well.

Despite these consequences, Americans do considerable borrowing. In 1984, there was over $1.8 trillion in mortgage debt outstanding on residential properties, which is about $8,000 per person. Consumer credit, such as auto loans and charge card balances, was nearly $600 billion or about $2,500 per person, including children. This means the average person is responsible for more than $1,000 in interest payments every year.

People incur debt because their needs, at least as they see them, exceed their current resources, but they believe they will have enough income to pay what is due when it is due. Corporations operate the same way when they borrow to enlarge their inventories and purchase new equipment.

The pressures on government officials are similar to those on corporations and individuals. When immediate needs seem to exceed immediate resources, borrowing can be an attractive course of action.

Americans have long feared that public officials will bow to public pressures to spend but avoid the criticism they would incur for raising taxes by running a deficit: that is, by borrowing the difference between revenues and spending. As a result of these concerns, the constitutions of practically every American state prohibit unbalanced operating budgets. Generally, state officials can borrow only to finance long-term capital outlays. In some states, even this requires direct voter approval. State laws keep our cities and counties from running unbalanced budgets as well.

5

Federal Borrowing

Our national government isn't bound by the same rules. Congress decides how much income the federal government will have by its decisions on tax laws. It decides how much will be spent by passing appropriation bills. Income doesn't necessarily equal outgo, causing deficits.

Public opinion surveys consistently show that Americans believe that the federal government should have a balanced budget. Our President says he supports a balanced budget. So did his opponent in the 1984 election and every major candidate in the primaries. Our state legislatures feel so strongly that over 30 of them have passed resolutions seeking an amendment to the Constitution to require that the federal budget be balanced.

Through most of American history, the federal government incurred deficits primarily to fight wars—operating on a balanced budget or surplus the rest of the time. From the founding of our nation until 1850, there was, on average, a surplus. In the following 50 years, which included the Civil War, the total 50-year deficit was under a billion dollars. (The deficit the federal government now incurs in two working days is larger than the entire deficit of those 50 years.) The government went about $22 billion in debt to finance World War I but wiped much of that out with surpluses in the 1920s.

The Great Depression of the 1930s was associated with deficits in those years, but never larger than $4.4 billion. Then came World War II, when the deficit reached $54 billion in the peak spending year. At the end of that war, our national debt was $260 billion. This total debt is about the same size as the annual deficits the nation is expected to run in the late 1980s. In the 1960s, the annual deficit was held to under $7 billion every year except at the peak of the Vietnam War, and there were surpluses in two years.

In the 1970s, deficits began to grow. In 1981, President Reagan proposed major tax cuts for individual citizens and corporations, which the Congress accepted with some changes. These cuts were in place during the early 1980s. It had been hoped that these tax cuts would so stimulate the economy that balanced budgets would be possible. Instead, the nation went into one of its worst recessions, which cut federal revenues while increasing spending. The result was large and growing deficits (Chart 1).

6

Chart 1. Federal Budget Deficits*

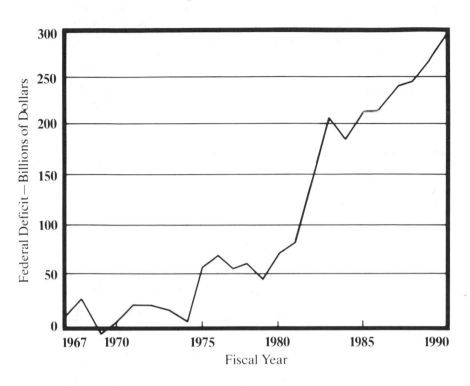

*Includes the "off-budget deficit items"

Source for 1985-1990 projections: Congressional Budget Office

The deficit is so large that to eliminate it in 1985 every worker in America would have to pay an additional $2,000 in taxes.

Future Deficits

Large deficits are now built into the federal budget. The projections in the chart above show what the Congressional Budget Office (CBO) predicts the deficit will be if Congress neither raises taxes nor alters current spending patterns. By 1990, revenues will be $1.088 trillion, but spending will be $1.384 trillion, leaving a deficit of $296 billion.

Different experts have different estimates concerning the magnitude of future deficits, but their numbers are all large. In early 1985, the Office of Management and Budget (OMB) estimated that continuing current services and taxes would produce a cumulative deficit of $1,181 billion during the five years beginning in October of 1985. A CBO estimate, made at about the same time, predicted $1,265 billion. Both these estimates assume there will be no recession during the five years or, if there is, that its effects will be canceled by a subsequent fast economic recovery. If our economy does not perform this well, deficits will be even larger.

The reasons for the red ink are simple. The President believes that we should return defense spending to roughly the same percentage of our GNP that it absorbed in the 1950s, which is considerably higher than the percentage prevailing in the late 1970s. The Congress has agreed to move in this direction. But spending for non-defense activities, particularly social security and health programs, has been taking an increasing share of our national output, and the 1981 tax cut reduced receipts from the 1980 level and kept revenues as a percentage of our GNP from rising significantly above the historical average. The table below shows what has been happening and what we can expect under current policies.

Table 1
Federal Finances in Relation to National Output (GNP):
Spending and Receipts as a Percentage of GNP

	Defense	Non-Defense	Total	Receipts
1950s Average	10.7%	7.5%	18.2%	17.8%
1960s Average	9.1	10.3	19.4	18.6
1970-1974 Average	7.0	13.0	20.0	18.8
1975-1979 Average	5.2	16.8	22.0	19.0
1985	6.5	17.8	24.3	19.1
1990 Projected	7.6	17.0	24.6	19.4

This table shows that spending has been increasing as a percentage of GNP, but since 1975 receipts (including payroll taxes) have been relatively stable, running between 19% and 20% of GNP.

The total national debt estimated for October 1, 1985, is $1.8 trillion. But the federal government itself holds a significant proportion of this debt in its trust funds, so most people focus on "debt held by the public," the concept used throughout this book. That debt estimate for October 1985 is $1.5 trillion.

With the debt this large, the interest bill is also large—$130 billion in fiscal year (FY) 1985. This bill will rise as each annual deficit makes the debt larger. It will also rise because old federal bonds were issued at low interest rates. When those bonds are paid off, the government will have to reborrow the money at the prevailing interest rate. In early 1985, that rate was 8.5% for short-term borrowing and 12% for bonds coming due in 30 years. Most estimates of future deficits assume that the short-term interest

8

rate will drop still further—to 6% or so by 1989. It may not. If it doesn't, interest costs and the federal deficits will be even larger.

The CBO projections show the impact of increasing interest costs as well as other factors affecting the budget on the percentage of GNP the deficit represents.

Chart 2. Federal Budget Deficits in Relation to GNP

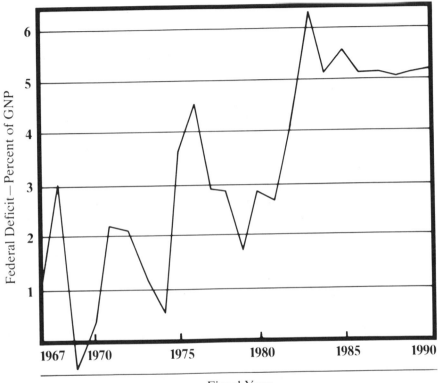

Fiscal Year

Source for 1985-1990 projections: Congressional Budget Office

The "Off-The-Books" Deficit

Most estimates of how much the federal government runs in the red don't include deficits carried in "off-budget" accounts. By law, the spending isn't included in the budget totals and thus doesn't affect the reported deficit. These items typically total from $10 billion to $20 billion a year.

A more serious omission is hidden liabilities for social security and other retirement programs. When a company has a pension plan, it is required to put aside money each year for its current workers to build up a fund for their retirement. This ensures that even if a company goes bankrupt, there is enough money set aside so that its retired workers will get their pensions. The federal government doesn't have a similar requirement for social security. Instead, the payroll taxes paid by workers and their employers are used to pay benefits to those already retired. Today's workers will have to get their pensions when they retire from those who are still working. If the federal government had to follow the practices it requires of private companies, the federal debt for pensions would be listed in the trillions.

The Size of the Debt

If current tax and spending policies are continued without change, the debt held by the public will grow to $2.8 trillion by October of 1990.

Chart 3. Federal Debt Held by the Public

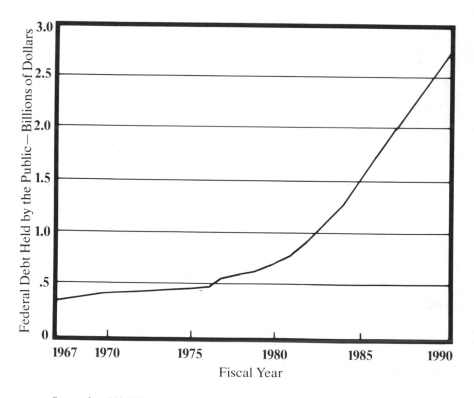

Fiscal Year

Source for 1985-1990 projections: Congressional Budget Office

One way to look at such a huge number is to allocate the debt to each worker in the United States. The October 1985 debt is estimated to be about $14,000 per worker. If current policies continue, it will rise to over $24,000 per worker by October of 1990.

Chart 4. Federal Debt Per Worker

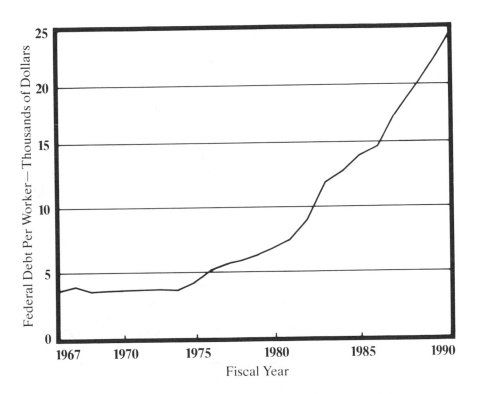

Based on debt projections by Congressional Budget Office and employment projections by the Roosevelt Center

The debt is like a good investment in reverse. A good investment compounds: it pays interest, which adds to the amount invested, which increases the interest, which further increases the amount invested, which increases the interest, and so on. The debt, on the other hand, creates interest costs which add to the principal owed, which increases the interest costs, which increases the principal owed, and so on. In 1985, each worker's share of the annual *interest* payments is about $1,400. If current policies are continued, the interest bill in 1990 will be about $2,000 per worker.

11

THE EFFECTS OF DEFICITS AND DEBT

The widespread impression that unbalanced federal budgets have become a way of life has triggered considerable interest in understanding the consequences of perpetual deficits and rising federal debt. While economists and others who have studied the subject don't agree completely on the details, all of them believe that a large government deficit has major impacts.

Deficits and the Business Cycle

One of the difficulties in having a balanced budget every year comes from the impact of business cycles—the periodic cycling of recession and rapid recovery that has characterized our economy for decades. During recessions, the federal budget suffers both a loss of revenues and increased spending. Slower growth in personal income means less revenue from the individual income tax; more unemployment means less social security payroll tax revenues; and corporate profits (and thus the tax on them) may actually decline in recession. On the spending side, high unemployment increases unemployment compensation costs as well as welfare spending. On the upswing, the experience is reversed. Spending pressures are reduced and revenues rise rapidly.

Many economists believe that these characteristics make the federal budget an ''automatic stabilizer'' of our economy—that is, they believe that deficits have different impacts depending on the state of the economy. In a recession, they argue, deficits are relatively harmless because there is plenty of money looking for borrowers. During such periods, having the government put more money into the economy (by spending) than it takes out (by taxing) can stimulate the economic recovery. But they fear deficits in prosperous times, because with our productive capacity fully in use, extra spending would raise prices, not production. They also fear that more government borrowing would ''crowd out'' borrowing important to growth, such as borrowing to finance new production facilities.

Other economists think that factors such as the overall level of taxes, the reach of regulatory policy, and the supply of money are the critical factors in economic growth and that deficits don't matter very much. Some of these people nevertheless oppose deficits for other reasons. For example, they think if the federal government is forced to balance its budget, this will tend to keep government spending and taxes low. But others are more willing to tolerate deficits.

One school of thought places great emphasis on the tax side of fiscal policy. High taxes are seen as the enemy of economic growth, and lower taxes are seen as stimulating so much private economic activity that added revenues from that activity might offset all or part of the deficit resulting from tax reduction. To persons taking this position, raising taxes is more of an evil than continuing to tolerate large deficits. They favor reducing deficits only through spending cuts. A related school of thought focuses on spending alone and decries the resources that are denied the private sector by public programs. This school does not emphasize the difference between financing this spending through taxes or through deficits.

Living on Credit

The main impact of debt on the finances of our government is like the impact of debt on the finances of a family. As is the case with family finances, why a debt is incurred has much to do with how burdensome the payments on it may become.

Most family debt is incurred to finance the one-time purchase of items that will provide enjoyment over a number of years. These debts have two important characteristics: (1) the value of the capital asset being financed exceeds the debt and (2) the debt is paid off on a schedule that normally means the asset will have some useful life after the debt is paid. This kind of debt can also be seen as a way of avoiding other costs by paying interest. For example, incurring the cost of interest on a mortgage saves the cost of paying rent.

If government followed this policy, it would borrow only to finance its investments in such things as federal dams, public buildings, and perhaps weapons. However, this is not why the federal government does most of its borrowing. Less than 12% of the federal budget is spent for these types of investments. The bulk of the budget goes for paying employees, financing social security benefits, making welfare payments, providing farm price subsidies, and extending grants to state and local governments. As a result, federal borrowing is less like family purchases of homes and cars and more analogous to a family that spends $2,000 a year more than it makes in order to pay rent and buy clothes, food, and entertainment.

Such a family can increase its living standard temporarily, particularly if it can get new loans to pay off old ones. But, in the second year, it would have to borrow $2,200—2,000 for another year of living beyond its income and $200 to pay interest on the first year's borrowing. Continuing on this course, the family would have to borrow more and more just to maintain its standard of living. Borrowing $2,000 a year to maintain a lifestyle, plus enough more each year to cover the interest, would result in interest costs of about $2,000 in the fifth year and $6,000 in the tenth year.

The math of compounding interest bills is much the same for governments.

13

Chart 5. Interest on the Federal Debt in Relation to GNP

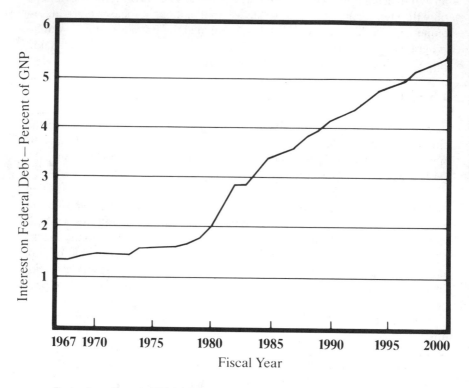

Projections through 1990 by Congressional Budget Office; those after 1990
by Roosevelt Center, using comparable assumptions

This chart shows that interest costs on the federal debt have been taking an increased share of our national output (GNP) since the early 1970s. Interest represented 1.4% of national output in FY 1973.

This had risen to 3.4% in FY 1985. The CBO predicts that it will rise to 4.1% by FY 1990. The Roosevelt Center carried these projections to FY 2000 and found that the interest bill would grow to about 5.4% of GNP, assuming continuation of current policies.

The CBO projections presume that real economic growth will continue at a favorable pace and that interest rates will remain moderate. If more pessimistic assumptions are used, the results are very different. The Roosevelt Center made projections based on the assumption that real GNP would grow at only 1% a year, inflation would remain at 5%, that the average interest rate on federal debt would be 11%, and that both federal revenues and spending (excluding interest) would remain the same percentage of GNP they are today.

This scenario produces results that most Americans would find unacceptable. Total federal spending would rise to 39% of GNP, up from 24% in 1984. Total federal debt soars to over $21 trillion at the end of 2005. This represents $168,000 for every American likely to be working in that year. Interest payments alone would be over $17,000 per worker. The scenario becomes totally impossible without tax increases by 2007. By then, all the taxes generated by keeping the current ratio of taxes to GNP must be used to pay interest with no money left even to pay the President and Congress.

This scenario may be unduly pessimistic, but the results have major similarity no matter which of the two sets of assumptions is used. Interest burdens grow over time for a government running constant operating deficits, just like they do for a family.

Families could not indefinitely maintain their lifestyle this way because before long, creditors would cease lending to them. The question is—is there any difference when government lives it up?

One difference is that our government has, everyone assumes, good credit, so it doesn't face the situation of being turned away by lenders as a bad risk. Neither a bank nor a friend would be likely to loan much money to a private party who wants to live beyond his means indefinitely. But the federal government has the legal ability to raise funds as needed.

Taxes are not automatic; however, lenders must believe that the decisionmakers in the White House and Congress have not only the power to tax but the willingness to use that power to raise taxes or cut non-interest spending (or both) in order to make interest payments. If this is doubted, the financial markets would demand much higher interest rates for loans to the federal government.

Another difference is that as the most creditworthy borrower, government can usually get a lower interest rate than the family discussed above. So its debt still skyrockets—but a little less rapidly.

Foreign Ownership of American Debt

Another difference, some say, is that we owe our debt to ourselves. Less than 20% of the federal debt is directly financed by loans from foreigners; the rest is owed to Americans. But the large deficits of the past several years are rapidly changing this relationship. In 1984, American finances became like those of a less developed country—we borrowed more from foreigners than we invested abroad. Some of our government borrowing from Americans was actually indirect borrowing from foreigners. For example, Arab oil money invested in a New York bank may finance that bank's loans to the federal government.

15

When Americans borrow from abroad, it's just like a family borrowing from a bank. The interest payments and any repayments of principal reduce the money available to live on. The larger the loans, the higher the share of income that must be used to pay the interest.

American Ownership of Federal Debt—Who Benefits and Who Pays

When the federal debt is financed by Americans, this export of interest abroad doesn't happen. Instead of siphoning money out of our economy, interest payments shift resources within our economy. But the people earning the interest are systematically different from the ones who are paying it.

Some federal debt is held by state and local governments investing temporarily idle funds; some by individuals; but most is held by institutions— banks, savings and loans, company pension plans, insurance companies, and industrial companies with money to invest. So the interest on debt goes primarily to these types of institutions.

To some extent, we all benefit from this interest if we have life insurance policies, private pension plans, or interest-bearing deposits in banks. But how much we benefit depends on how large our stakes are. Those who benefit most are the ones who own stock in banks and other financial institutions, large depositors, and those with large pensions and life insurance policies. Personal net worth provides a good index of relative benefits. That is, on average, one would expect someone with net worth of half a million to receive about 100 times as much from federal interest payments as someone with a net worth of $5,000. Many Americans have negligible (or even negative) net worth.

Rather than saying that we owe the federal debt to ourselves, it is more accurate to say that the debt is, on balance, owed by those who pay federal taxes (now and in the future) to those who already have wealth. In short, it is owed by taxpayers to bondholders.

16

The table below shows shares of payments of federal income tax in 1982 in relation to adjusted gross income. Clearly, the bulk of tax funds is raised from middle-income taxpayers.

Table 2

Income Tax Revenues by Income Group

Adjusted Gross Income	Percentage of Total Federal Income Tax Paid by this Group
0-11,000	3.4
11-22,000	14.7
22-35,000	24.9
35-50,000	21.3
50-100,000	18.2
100-200,000	7.9
200-1,000,000	6.9
Over 1,000,000	2.7

The table does not include social security payroll taxes. Because there is a limit on the amount of income subject to this tax; no progressivity in rate; and no deductions, exemptions, or credits for this tax, poorer persons pay a larger proportion of their incomes in tax than those making over $40,000 a year.

You can figure where you stand personally by thinking about your tax return last year. To begin with, you had direct gains and losses from interest payments. Your income from capital (investment) is what you received in interest and dividends. Your payment for capital (debt) is what you paid in interest.

You also paid and received interest indirectly. Assuming earmarked taxes like social security don't pay interest costs, about one-fourth of your federal income tax went to pay interest on the federal debt. If you rent, much of your payment covers your owner's interest costs. But you had interest gains that don't appear on your tax form from appreciation in life insurance policies with cash value, from individual retirement accounts (IRAs) and Keogh plans, and from private pension reserves.

Intergenerational Effects

Higher interest on growing federal debt has important implications for the living standards of younger and older persons.

Young workers just starting out in life tend to be borrowers. Many borrow to finance their education, borrow again for a car, go deeply into debt to buy a house if they can, then face the massive costs of raising children. Most are

17

hard pressed financially until the children leave home. By then, their salaries have risen, their mortgages are close to being paid off, and their obligations to their children have decreased. At this point, these people have money to lend. Their savings are encouraged by the government through such provisions as the special tax treatment of capital gains and IRAs. (These devices provide no help, of course, to those hard-pressed people who still need all their income to pay current living expenses.) Thus, higher interest rates tend to transfer resources from younger to older workers.

When people retire, all of their income is derived from payment on capital in some form—rent for any property they own, dividends on stocks, interest on bonds and money funds, and income from investments in company pension plans. Anything that tends to increase interest rates, which deficits are believed to do, will increase the flow of money from younger to older persons.

Effects on Federal Programs

So long as the government spends more than it takes in, interest costs will continue to rise, making it harder and harder to avoid future deficits. One reaction to this is increased pressure on Congress to scale back other programs. The nation witnessed this in 1985 with serious consideration being given to cutting spending important to social security recipients, state and local officials, farmers, and others.

Deficits and Interest Rates

When the government finances its deficit by borrowing large sums, it comes into competition with other borrowers. These include business trying to expand plants and finance inventories, and people seeking to finance their homes and cars.

All these potential borrowers are bidding for the opportunity to make use of capital set aside by potential lenders. These include people who save some of their money in bank deposits, savings and loan shares, certificates of deposit, and bonds. Businesses also save when they establish pension funds and when they pay out less in dividends and building new facilities than their cash flow. State and local governments save through their retirement funds. Insurance companies are also major savers because they collect money now to cover payments that often don't have to be made for many years.

Clearly, it is impossible to borrow more than the total capital available. It is interest rates that equalize the amounts borrowed and lent. If more people want to save than borrow, interest rates will drop. This drop encourages more people to borrow and fewer to save. On the other hand, if there are more borrowers than lenders, interest rates will tend to rise, discouraging borrowing.

Assume that the economy is operating normally with no federal deficit. Some people would be borrowing and some lending. Of course, the amount saved would be the same as the amount borrowed. Now imagine that the federal government decides to run a deficit of $200 billion a year, thereby increasing what would otherwise be borrowed in the total economy by a third to a half.

The federal decision to borrow $200 billion will not automatically cause anyone to save more. People will not alter their savings for retirement, down payments, or college educations merely because a deficit is announced. Corporate cash flow will not be increased, nor will contributions to pension plans or to IRAs.

With more demand to borrow without more money to lend, interest rates will have to rise to scare off some of the potential borrowers and encourage more saving. But it's hard to get people and companies to save more just because the interest rate is a little higher:

- People don't often change their payroll deductions for savings or take fewer vacations just because interest rates rise a little.
- The government deficit doesn't make company profits any higher nor dividends any lower, so company savings, in the short run at least, will not respond to higher interest rates.
- Pension commitments of employers are unchanged and so are the schedules by which they accumulate money in pension plans.

One of the major effects of high interest rates in encouraging savings occurs quite slowly. Many people automatically reinvest their interest. This happens in savings accounts, money funds, and dividend reinvestment plans. When they collect higher interest, they reinvest more money. But this effect is gradual.

For the most part, therefore, the balancing of borrowing and lending comes about not by increasing the savings rate, but rather by driving off some of the potential borrowers through higher interest rates. This happens quickly for some borrowers. The willingness of a mortgage company to extend a housing loan depends on whether loan officers think a potential borrower can pay. They decide this by comparing income to the mortgage payment. Higher interest rates make the mortgage payment higher without increasing income, so some people lose their chance to get a mortgage. Higher rates also discourage investment because they increase the costs of holding rental housing and inventories and financing new plants without increasing the expected profits.

Effects of High Interest Rates

High interest rates have very different effects on people in different situations, even when the economy as a whole is performing nicely. To make a long story short, they explain why many people are out of work in the lumber industry in Oregon, the textile industry in the Carolinas, and the steel industry in the Midwest.

High rates get people more interested in how they invest their money and tend to create more employment in places like banks and brokerage houses. However, they discourage people from making new housing purchases, which tends to create unemployment among housing contractors and in the lumber industry. They also discourage buying financed by loans—new cars, boats, and second homes. Potential buyers decide whether to purchase by looking at the monthly payment. The higher the interest rate, the higher the monthly payment.

Because high rates discourage investment, they also hurt the industries that provide what business invests in—the contractors who construct new plants, the machine tool makers, and those who build heavy trucks and farm equipment.

Deficits and American Trade

For the reasons discussed above, interest rates will tend to rise when the federal government runs a large deficit, but savings won't respond very much. Borrowers get squeezed out of the market, but they may still be able to borrow if they can get money from outside the country. Companies can borrow in the Eurobond market and can have their foreign subsidiaries raise their capital abroad. Individual Americans do not borrow abroad directly. But they do so indirectly when European and Japanese banks come to this country and make loans here, as well as when foreign investors buy American mortgages from federal agencies and mortgage bankers. The federal government itself also borrows abroad when, for example, foreigners buy Treasury securities.

During most of the 20th century, foreign lending to Americans has been less than American investments in foreign countries. However, if the deficit causes American interest rates to increase, more than the usual numbers of foreigners will want to invest here to get the higher return on their money. Higher interest rates are not, however, the only cause of this recent surge of foreign capital into our country. Some foreigners feel that property in their own country might be confiscated after political upheavals, so they hold assets here. Many also feel that the dollar is a more stable currency than their own—less subject to fluctuation or to deliberate inflation that could wipe out the value of their investments.

20

This foreign money is, in effect, extra money for our economy. It tends to promote economic activity and keep interest rates from rising even farther. The bad news is that the money must eventually be repaid, with interest. Those payments will reduce American living standards when they are made, just as paying off a consumer loan does. Thus, many people view with alarm the fact that more capital now appears to be flowing into the United States than American firms and individuals are investing abroad.

There are other problems as well. Our high interest rates tend to draw lending to our government, companies, and individuals by people holding their money in yen, marks, pounds, and other foreign currencies. To make dollar-denominated investments, they need to convert these currencies to dollars. With more people trying to buy dollars and sell foreign currencies, the value of the dollar increases relative to those currencies. This makes goods of other countries (our imports) cheaper in our country and makes our goods more expensive in other countries, hampering our exports. Since 1980, the dollar has appreciated 38% in relation to major foreign currencies, as shown in Chart 6.

Chart 6. Value of the Dollar in Relation to Foreign Currencies

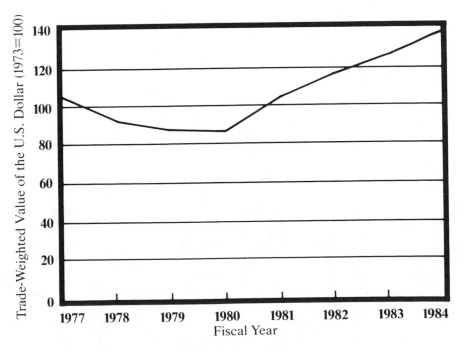

Source: *Economic Report of the President, 1985*

21

This in turn means that our imports tend to increase while our exports don't grow to match. The result is shown in Chart 7.

Chart 7. U.S. Merchandise Trade Deficit

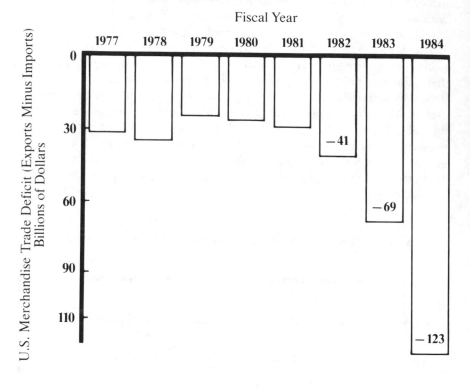

Source: 1977-1983, *Economic Report of the President;*
1984, *Survey of Current Business*

Americans buy more Japanese cars, more Korean textiles, and more vacations in Mexico. Brazilians buy fewer U.S. cars and shoes and more from their own companies and from other countries. Businesses respond just like people. American manufacturers start buying foreign steel. People with construction contracts in Africa buy their construction machinery from a Japanese competitor, not Caterpillar Tractor.

What does this mean in jobs? If we assume $45,000 of production means about one American job, then Americans lost over 7 million jobs because of imports in 1984. But we gained nearly 5 million jobs because we sell to other countries. The difference—over two million jobs—is the cost of the trade deficit.

22

Those two million jobs are from companies losing out in the export markets, like Caterpillar's laid-off employees, and hundreds of thousands of laid-off auto, steel, and textile workers who lost out to imports. But other people's jobs are affected as well because the income from those lost jobs once created jobs for others such as city employees, fast food workers, and retail clerks. This means roughly another two million jobs are involved.

In simple terms, the United States has been importing other people's money at the price of exporting American jobs.

More on Deficits and Interest Rates

It seems logical that if government tries to borrow more and nothing else changes, interest rates would tend to rise. That's the view of most economists, along with most of our national political, labor, and business leaders. But not everyone agrees. Those who want to consider this issue in more detail will want to read this section.

Interest rates are affected by many different factors. One of the most important is how our economy is performing. When the economy is booming, everybody wants to borrow. Consumers are confident and want to borrow; businesses need more inventory and are confident they can sell more if they invest in new plants and equipment. Thus, interest rates usually rise in times of economic recovery. In recession, the reverse happens. Business and consumers are afraid to borrow, and rates tend to fall.

Interest rates are also influenced by expectations of inflation. Generally speaking, lenders seek a rate of return that will compensate them for anticipated rates of inflation and yield a real return. If lenders expect prices to be stable, they may lend money at a rate of something like 3%, as people did in the 1950s. But if they expect inflation of 10% a year, they will need an interest rate of 13% to get the same 3% return adjusted for inflation. If interest payments result in taxable income, they will need an even higher rate in the inflationary environment to match the 3% in a non-inflationary environment. And if the rate of inflation appears volatile and unpredictable, lenders will also demand a "risk premium" as compensation.

Because of these and other factors, no one expects changes in interest rates to mirror precisely any one factor, such as the size of the deficit. Data from one point in time showing the interest rate with a deficit and the interest rate without one would be reasonably conclusive. But at any point in time, there is either a big deficit or there isn't, so this controlled experiment can never be performed. Instead, economists create statistical models of how the economy behaves and ask these models what would happen if the deficits were different. These models generally show that higher deficits mean higher interest rates, but there will never be a way to prove conclusively that the models are accurate.

Chart 8 shows the relationship between two key measures of interest rates. The top line is the interest rate on 91-day bills, which the Treasury uses as one of the major ways to finance the deficit. This is also about the rate which banks would pay on certificates of deposit. Other rates (e.g., bank loans) are higher because they involve more risk and administrative costs for the banks.

These rates that borrowers actually pay are known as ''nominal'' interest rates.

The bottom line shows the ''real'' rate of interest, defined as the difference between the inflation rate and the nominal interest rate. It is the lender's annual gain in purchasing power.

Chart 8. Nominal and Real Interest Rates

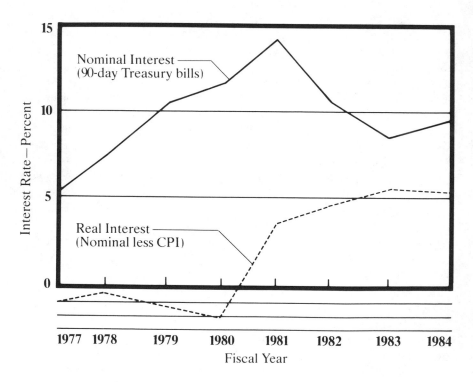

Source: Calculated by the Roosevelt Center

Thus, while the nominal interest rate in 1984 was well below levels of earlier years, those who lend money were getting much better real returns in 1983 and 1984 than just about any time in our history. This doesn't prove that high real rates are caused by current big deficits, but it is certainly consistent with that theory.

Summary: Deficits are Important

- They increase the national debt.
  - —Higher debt causes higher federal interest expenses, making it more difficult to balance the budget the next year.
  - —Higher debt must ultimately force higher taxes, cutbacks in federal spending, or both.
  - —Higher debt causes bigger drains on the American economy to pay interest to people and institutions in other countries.
- They tend to drive up interest rates.
  - —Higher interest rates move private money from those that don't have much to those who have the most—from young to old, and from poor and middle class to rich.
  - —Higher interest rates discourage the business investment needed for economic growth.
  - —Higher interest rates encourage foreigners to lend us money, making the dollar more valuable, which worsens our balance of trade and costs Americans their jobs.

But just because deficits have harmful effects doesn't mean anything will be, or should be, done about them. Both tax increases (discussed in Chapter 3) and spending cuts (discussed in Chapter 4) inflict pain and damage on substantial portions of our population. And, just as important, there is little agreement among politicians, economists, and average citizens as to the most appropriate approach to the task of deficit reduction.

GETTING OUT FROM UNDER FEDERAL DEBT

It is not easy for a government, particularly a stable one, to get out from under its debt and the burdens it creates for its people. Occasionally, after a revolution, a government will repudiate debt. However, this is surprisingly infrequent because the new leaders recognize that lenders are not likely to extend new loans to a country that acts in this fashion. It would be almost unthinkable for a country like the United States to do so. Politically, there would be massive problems with American citizens who would have their Treasury bonds rendered worthless by decree. Economically, a government that had repudiated its debt could hardly expect to go back to those it had injured and ask them to advance such a government more money.

25

Yet repudiation could start to be considered seriously as new generations of Americans become increasingly restive over the immense debt burdens shifted to them by prior generations. While direct repudiation of national debt along the lines portrayed in the first chapter is unlikely, governments can (as some foreign governments do) seek to reduce the burden of debt indirectly by inflation.

The Inflation "Solution"

There is one simple way to deal with the burden of debt on the younger generation—inflation.

Take a 30-year-old couple with income of $35,000. Such a couple might have a debt of $65,000 for a house, $5,000 for a car, $3,000 on credit cards, and (what they don't see but must shoulder through taxes) a $24,000 share of the federal debt. All told, this is $97,000 in debt. To pay interest alone through taxes, mortgage and car payments, and monthly credit card bills, they would need $11,640, or nearly a third of their income.

But what if the government quickly expanded the money supply, in effect printing more money, adding one new dollar for each old one? This would immediately cause adjustments in wages and prices which would be about equal, so the couple wouldn't gain or lose from that. However, they would now have income of $70,000, and their interest costs would drop from a third of their income to a sixth. Paying off their debt would also be less burdensome—taking a little more than a year instead of almost three if the couple could somehow devote all their income to paying it off. This simple example illustrates why inflation is the ally of the debtor and the enemy of the creditor. As the federal government goes deeper and deeper in debt, deliberate inflation, many fear, will be increasingly attractive. Unlike direct repudiation, an acceleration of inflation will penalize all creditors, not just those who own government securities. Creditors who had lent money at fixed rates for a long term would be penalized because they could not adjust their interest rates to compensate.

Government can create additional money in complex ways, mainly by regulating banks and by purchasing and selling securities held by the Federal Reserve Banks. One cause of inflation is increasing the amount of money in circulation faster than the economy grows. Some nations, most recently Argentina, Brazil, and Israel, deliberately do this, partly to cut the burdens of their domestic debt. This results in rapid increases—sometimes at triple-digit rates. Thus far, the United States has avoided such hyper-inflation. Inflation has rarely been more than 10% a year. In the last several years, annual price inflation has been under 5%.

Inflation has many nasty side effects. As prices spiral, some people can't get their wages increased fast enough to keep up. People with fixed incomes, such as private pension plan retirees, are particularly hard hit.

26

But the worst effects of inflation appear when people come to expect more and more inflation. They tend to spend their money quickly because they know that houses, art, precious metals and other durables will gain in value while money will lose. This tends to drive up prices even faster. Interest rates also tend to rise as people avoid lending money for long periods unless they are confident that their return will be enough to cover reduced purchasing power.

CONCEPTS OF AN ACCEPTABLE DEFICIT

The consequences of an immediate move to balance the budget are not acceptable to many American political leaders. The consequences of continued deficits in the hundreds of billions of dollars, even in economic recovery, are unacceptable to most of them, too. Many of these leaders have tried, therefore, to define the "appropriate deficit path."

The path can be viewed as the annual deficits (as dollars or percentage of GNP) moving over time. The idea is that this line should be heading downward. There is disagreement over whether the end point should be a surplus, a balanced budget, or a smaller deficit. There are also disagreements over the speed with which this target is to be reached.

Some alternative paths are discussed below.

End Deficits and Run Enough Surplus to Pay Off the Debt

This concept considers the impact of debt to be so serious as to merit not only balanced budgets but also repayment of the federal debt as quickly as possible.

However, substantial surpluses could slow economic growth by lowering demand for goods below our capacity to produce them. Income taxes used to pay off debt would draw funds from taxpayers who would otherwise spend practically all those funds in ways that would stimulate overall economic activity. Repayment of debt would be made to persons and institutions (e.g., foreigners, financial institutions, pension funds, wealthy individuals) who would be unlikely to use much of the money for consumption.

One obvious solution to this problem is to finance repayment of the debt out of accumulated wealth rather than incomes. Taxes with this effect include estate and gift taxes and a possible new tax based upon wealth. The other possibility is to run the big surpluses only when the economy is overheating, that is, when taking money out of the economy helps long-term growth.

Perpetually Balanced Budgets

Balanced budgets mandated by Constitutional amendment would end the deficit problem in the future without addressing the problem of accumulated past debt. Debt would remain constant while the nation's GNP increased as a result of real growth and inflation. As a result, the percentage of GNP represented by debt and annual interest payments would steadily drop until, after several generations, it became negligible. This path would reduce the burden of debt and interest payments over time.

A Balanced Budget Over the Business Cycle: The traditional Keynesian view calls for the budget to be balanced over the business cycle, running deficits in recessions to spur recovery and surpluses during rapid expansions to block overheating. This approach would call for surpluses in years of higher-than-average growth, such as 1984. There are substantial practical problems with this approach. It assumes economists can predict recession and recovery and that political leaders will be willing to run surpluses rather than distribute them through tax relief and higher spending.

A Full Employment Balance: Another approach would seek a balanced "full employment budget." That is, there would be no deficit or surplus when the economy was performing at full capacity. This approach would call for deficits when the economy was performing at less than full capacity.

The "Tolerable" Deficit

The concept of the tolerable deficit is that there is a point (measured as a percentage of GNP) where deficits are small enough to be tolerable. At that point, the detrimental effects of deficits (e.g., higher interest rates) become small enough so that they neither cause massive dislocations of economic activity nor sow the seeds for subsequent recession or depressed growth patterns. The number most often mentioned in association with this concept is 2% of GNP.

The setting of a tolerable deficit target does not involve a threshold under which everything is good and nothing is bad and over which nothing is good and everything is bad. Instead, it is a continuum along several dimensions. For example, if the tolerable deficit is set at 2.1% rather than 2.0%, interest rates would be expected to be slightly higher, the dollar somewhat stronger, exports somewhat less, imports somewhat greater, and so forth. On the other hand, taxes would be lower, expenditures higher, or both.

Factors that might be taken into consideration in defining a "tolerable deficit" could include historical deficit patterns, deficit levels in other countries, one's preferences for spending and tax levels, and as many other factors as there are effects of deficits.

Constant Debt Burden

Another approach would be to freeze the national debt as a percentage of GNP. This would allow total debt to rise at the same rate as GNP. For example, GNP is expected to rise by 9.4% in 1985. Debt, which will be about $1.4 trillion at the beginning of 1985 could be allowed to rise by 9.4% or $132 billion. This would mean a deficit of 3.3% of GNP. Given stable interest rates, such a course would also freeze interest costs as a percentage of GNP. While freezing the problems associated with debt, however, this policy would not solve problems associated with deficits.

Attempting to Achieve a Particular Quantity of Investment

Another approach to deciding how much debt to tolerate as a percentage of GNP is to set investment targets, assume savings and flows of foreign capital, and see how much "room" is left for a federal deficit.

The choice of a target investment level is somewhat arbitrary. Because the years 1977 through 1979 were relatively good ones, the average investment (business and housing combined) level of those years, 17.4% of GNP, could be taken as the target. Saving by households, businesses, and state and local governments has been quite stable as a combined total, averaging 18.3% of GNP over the past seven years. With zero financing by foreigners, this would suggest "room" for a federal deficit of 0.9% of GNP, or about $32 billion in 1985. To make room for a larger deficit, it would be necessary, given a fixed investment target, either to increase business, personal, and local government savings or to borrow from abroad.

However, the natural economic force of higher interest rates cannot cause the necessary change in savings while preserving the target level of investment. As noted earlier, savings behavior tends to be much more insensitive to interest rate changes than business investment and consumer borrowing to purchase housing. Thus, ways would have to be found to encourage more saving by consumers and businesses while not increasing interest rates. One way to do that would be through changes in tax laws.

Summary of Longer-Term Deficit Approaches

The table below summarizes the long-term approaches to deficits. The final alternative discussed above is insufficiently specific for inclusion.

Table 3
Summary of Alternative Deficit Strategies

Strategy	Budget Condition in time of:			Change in Debt over time:	
	Recession	Normal Growth	Over-heating	Absolute Amount	As % of GNP
Pay off Debt	Surplus or Balanced	Surplus	Surplus	Reduced	Reduced
Balanced Budget	Balanced	Balanced	Balanced or Surplus	Reduced	Reduced
Balance Over Cycle	Deficit	Balanced	Surplus	Stable	Reduced
Full Employment Balance	Deficit	Deficit*	Balanced* or Surplus	Increased	Probably Reduced
Tolerable Deficit	Deficit	Deficit	Deficit	Increased	Depends on Plan
Stable Burden	Deficit	Deficit	Deficit	Increased	Stable

*If a normally growing economy is assumed not to have full employment, this concept allows a deficit during normal growth.

The Glide Path

Advocates of these various patterns realize that large deficits are built into current polices and that massive changes in spending and/or taxes would be required to eliminiate deficits in one year. Thus, they seek a pattern of deficit reduction that moves towards their eventual goal over several years.

Many consider this gradual ("glide path") approach appropriate because most of the deficit-correction measures have deficit-reducing impacts that increase from year to year. For example, holding down social security costs by subtracting 1% from the cost-of-living increases saves about 1% in the first year, 2% in the second, and so forth. Reducing the rate of increase in defense spending compounds in this way also, as does ending indexing of individual income taxes. The effect of many other measures also grows, albeit less rapidly.

Chapter Three

Raising Revenues

There are three ways of looking at what the finances of the federal government should be. The first way is to specify how high taxes should be and then consider how to spend within that ceiling. The second is to decide how much should be spent and then consider how to raise enough to cover the outlays. The third is to look at both at once, reconsidering tentative views on one in light of their effects on the other.

Where the Government Gets its Money

The chart below shows where the federal government gets its revenues, as projected for FY 1990.[1]

---

1. Most of the federal budget numbers used in these chapters are for FY 1990. The numbers reflect the Congressional Budget Office's projection of what spending and revenues in FY 1990 would be if the policies of 1985 were carried out unchanged through that year. It is not realistic to expect that Congress will take steps in one year that will balance the budget in that year. Too much spending is already committed—weapons are being produced under past contracts, many housing subsidies are locked in by past contracts, and so on. When Congress makes tax law changes, it typically gives taxpayers time to adjust to them. So national leaders concerned with the deficit are looking for a path of deficit reduction that would progressively cut the deficit more each year. FY 1990 was selected as one of several points where such a path could reach its chosen target.

31

Chart 9. Revenue Sources—Fiscal Year 1990

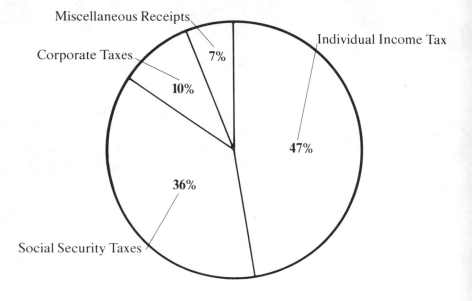

Source: Congressional Budget Office

Most of the money comes from taxes on individuals. This individual income tax is the government's biggest source of revenues, raising 47% of the total. The social security (FICA) tax raises 36%, split equally between employees and their employers. Taxes on corporate income raise a little less than 10% of revenues. Miscellaneous receipts such as customs revenues and excise taxes make up the remaining 7%.

The Burdens of Federal Taxes

In every society, taxes tend to be disliked. First, they are involuntary and people resent not having any choice about paying them. Second, practically any tax system is going to seem unfair to someone. Third, not everyone likes each of the many different ways that governments spend their money.

Regardless of the merit of these views, it is clear that taxes affect our economy by reducing the total amount of money available for private consumption and investment. Taxes also affect the economy by altering patterns of consumption and investment. When people give a little extra to charity because it is deductible, open IRAs for the tax savings, or buy tax-exempt bonds, and when corporations purchase equipment to take advantage of "accelerated depreciation" or buy other corporations for their "tax loss carryforward," the overall shape of our economy is changed to some extent.

The pressure for distortions is particularly intense when tax rates are high. In our income tax system, the key rate is what taxpayers pay on an added dollar of income or save from an added dollar of deductions (the "marginal rate"). For example, someone with income of $50,000 will have a marginal rate of about 43%. This creates strong incentives for such individuals to seek tax shelters and to avoid reporting income by working "off the books."

Besides encouraging tax shelters, it can be argued that high tax rates discourage people from working and investing because of the high percentage of the proceeds taken away by government. Taxes on American corporations are often cited as one reason why American companies have difficulty competing with companies from other countries.

How High are Taxes Now?

There are many ways to measure the level of taxation. One widely accepted way is to relate taxes to the total output of our economy—the gross national product or GNP. On this basis, federal taxes have been around 20% for some time, but were lower at earlier periods in our history and higher in wartime. The relationship between federal taxes and GNP is shown below for the period FY 1967-1985.

Chart 10. Federal Revenues in Relation to GNP

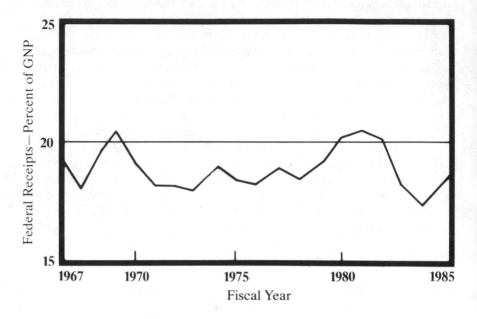

Federal Receipts— Percent of GNP

25

20

15

1967   1970   1975   1980   1985

Fiscal Year

Some people believe that the way to deal with federal government finances is to set a ceiling on this number, so federal taxes can never rise above 20% or so of GNP. With spending what it is now, doing this would mean either continued substantial deficits or major spending reductions. Some state governments do have constitutional limits on how high their taxes or spending can go in relation to the size of their total economies. But many opponents argue that such limits would be impractical for the federal government because it must be able to deal with expensive crises, such as major wars.

Ways to Raise Taxes

There are several ways that more money could be raised from our existing tax system. The most obvious way is simply to raise current tax rates. For example, a "surcharge" might be imposed. People would calculate their

34

taxes as they do now and then add another five or ten percent to their tax bills.

Another way would be to end what is known as "indexing." For decades Congress has been able to provide major reductions in federal tax rates every few years while continuing to raise more revenues. The explanation for this anomalous state of affairs was the effect of inflation on individual taxpayers.

Our federal income tax is actually a succession of different rates associated with different income levels (known as "brackets"). We pay zero percent on part of our income because it is offset by our personal exemptions and itemized deductions. Income above that is taxed in different brackets. For example, in 1985 a married couple would pay 14% on their taxable income between $7,910 and $12,390, 16% on income between $12,391 and $16,650 and so on up to a tax of 50% of income over $169,020.

Now consider the impact of inflation on taxes over time. Suppose a couple had taxable income of $34,100 in 1984 and got a raise of 5%—about equal to inflation. Assuming their deductions remained the same, their taxes would go from $7,507 to $8,155, an increase of 8.6% as compared to a salary increase of 5%. This would happen because all of their raise would be taxed at 38%, much higher than their average tax of 22% on the income they were earning before. Many people didn't like this because it encouraged federal spending and made people pay a higher fraction of their income to government each year even though their purchasing power didn't go up.

To correct this situation, Congress passed a law establishing indexation, which adjusts the brackets for inflation each year, starting in 1985. The result is that the "inflation tax" is gone, but so is the automatic growth in federal revenues that helped prevent big deficits in the past. One alternative would be to go back to the old system—at least for as long as it would take to eliminate deficits. One objection to either imposing a surcharge or repealing indexing is that it would cause people's marginal tax rates to rise, thereby magnifying economic distortions.

New Taxes

Some people would like to see the United States enact new taxes to close the deficit, to reduce the rates and burdens of some current taxes, or both.

There are three things governments can tax—income, consumption, and assets. Currently, the federal system relies almost totally on taxing income.

State and local governments use asset taxes, with the local property tax being the most significant. Occasionally someone proposes that the federal government tax wealth, but these proposals are not being given very serious consideration at the moment.

Serious consideration has been given in some quarters to the idea of national consumption taxes. By taxing income, the United States makes people pay taxes on income used for savings and investment. The argument is that if the federal government taxed money only when people spent it for consumption, people would tend to save and invest more to finance long-run economic growth.

There are three ways to tax consumption. One is the way the states do it now—a sales tax calculated as a certain percentage of the price of anything purchased, with the money collected at the cash register. Another way to get about the same result is a value-added tax, used by many European countries. This tax is paid by the manufacturers and wholesalers, not the customer. However, everyone agrees that the customer pays in the end, so the economic impact of value-added and sales taxes is similar.

One advantage of sales, and particularly value-added, taxes is that enforcement is easier than with an income tax. The tax is built into the price of the product under a value-added tax, so the retailer has no choice but to reflect it in the final price. With a sales tax, the tax is added separately, but the records of most retailers are so comprehensive that it is nearly impossible for them to avoid paying the tax.

One consequence of such taxes is that the less money people make, the higher the percentage of their income is paid as tax. Although everyone is taxed at the same rate, poor people tend to spend a greater proportion of their income than rich people, so they would pay taxes at a higher rate. If an income tax were retained, this impact could be offset by dropping income tax rates more in the low brackets than in the high ones. Alternatively, a wide range of goods, such as food, making up the bulk of purchases among poorer people, could be exempted from consumption taxation altogether.

A consumption or expenditure tax could also be collected using the system now used to collect the income tax. Income would be about what it is now, except that taxpayers would have to add in any money they take out of past investments. Items such as interest on home mortgages and sales taxes would no longer be deductible. But money put into savings and investments would be. This tax could be a flat rate, or it could have graduated rates—the higher the consumption, the higher the rate.

Another possibility is taxing selected items people consume. The federal government already has such taxes on alcohol, tobacco, and telephone services, in addition to taxes on gasoline to finance roads and on airplane tickets to finance airports.

One proposal that has been seriously advocated from time to time over the past decade is some sort of excise tax on energy. The most comprehensive approach would tax the value of all energy consumed. Such a tax is viewed as likely to promote energy conservation efforts and reduce American reliance on Arab oil supplies. A narrower approach would be just to tax imported oil. However, some political leaders in the East object to this because it would increase energy prices in the East (which gets oil from abroad)

36

while leaving prices in the West (which uses mostly domestic oil) unchanged.

Another variant on the energy tax idea is to place much higher taxes on gasoline, which many European nations do. Besides raising money, such a tax would encourage Americans to drive smaller, more fuel-efficient cars and discourage people from selecting jobs and residences at locations requiring long commutes. Sudden imposition of such an increase would, however, create some hardships for persons now committed to larger cars or long commutes.

Another suggestion is that taxes be sharply raised on products that are considered harmful to health, such as alcohol and tobacco. Opponents of these proposals argue that such taxes take a greater share of the income of poor persons than richer ones. They also note that higher taxes may discourage people from using these substances, but if they do, they won't raise much money, particularly if some of the production goes underground and escapes tax.

Reforming Current Taxes

In recent years, the idea of retaining but reforming our current corporate and personal income taxes has been widely discussed.

For taxes on individuals, the idea most frequently discussed is broadening the tax base. This means making the income subject to tax correspond more closely to income as people commonly define it when considering how much their neighbors and associates make. At present, there are big differences, including:

- Transactions that produce income not counted in the income reported for federal taxes. Examples are interest on state and local bonds; 60% of capital gains; most capital gains on the sale of one's home; and fringe benefits such as retirement plans, life insurance, and expensive business meals.
- Items that reduce income through deductions such as state and local taxes, certain medical expenses and casualty losses, and contributions to charity.

There are also many items that reduce taxes by providing credits (dollar-for-dollar offsets) against taxes owed. Examples are investments in home energy conservation measures, payments for child care, and political contributions.

For corporations, there is a wide deviation among three notions of income: cash flow, income reported to shareholders, and income reported to the Internal Revenue Service. Reform ideas involve closing some of this gap.

37

Cash flow is simply how much a corporation takes in minus what it pays out to employees and suppliers. There is little interest in basing the federal taxes on it because corporations with large investment expense would pay no taxes even though they report earnings.

The difference between income reported to shareholders and income reported for federal tax purposes stems mostly from what is known as depreciation. Everyone concerned with tax policy agrees that corporations should be able to consider the money they invest in new facilities and equipment as expenses. The question is when. Corporations report capital outlays to stockholders as expenses while the asset is being used up. For example, if a truck is expected to last ten years, a corporation might report one-tenth of its value as depreciation expense in each of ten years. But the federal tax law allows them to charge off this truck in three years. This allows them to show higher expenses in the first three years, reducing income. As long as corporations keep making big investments, this effectively reduces the income on which they are taxed.

Moving to a broader concept of income would massively increase the amount of income that companies and individuals report as being subject to tax. If no other changes were made, this would mean a significant increase in federal tax revenue. Thus, broadening the tax base could permit a dramatic lowering of tax rates. For example, for individuals, all of the revenue now produced by income taxes with rates up to 50% could be produced by a broader tax base and a rate of 14% of income applicable to everyone—in effect, a flat tax. However, many people like the idea that persons with higher incomes should be taxed at a higher rate than lower incomes, so they favor preserving the graduated tax.

The idea of broadening what is counted as income and dramatically reducing rates while keeping rates higher for higher incomes has recently been proposed in a widely publicized study by the U.S. Treasury Department. Some Members of Congress have introduced bills along the same lines.

While the principle of broadening the tax base and reducing rates is widely accepted, each provision of current tax law has its own set of defenders. Many business leaders contend that rapid depreciation and investment credits are necessary to encourage needed investment and create jobs. Recipients of charitable contributions (churches, universities and others) contend that if such contributions are not deductible, people will reduce their giving. State and local officials contend that taking away the deductibility of their taxes would make it harder for them to raise revenue at a time when many responsibilities are being shifted to them from the federal government. Every deduction, credit, and exclusion from income was placed in the tax code because someone made enough of a case for it to convince a majority in Congress. This suggests that removing these special provisions would not be easy.

People recommending tax reform typically structure their proposals to raise exactly as much money as the present tax system. However, it would be possible to design plans that combined a reformed tax structure with higher revenues that could be used to close the deficit.

More Minor Changes

Congress may not choose either to raise rates of existing taxes or to launch a massive reform and restructuring of the nation's tax system. If it doesn't, it could still raise substantial amounts by adopting some reforms in the form of less dramatic piecemeal changes. As might be expected, such changes tend to affect a relatively small number of people (whose taxes would be raised). The changes are both easier for Congress to adopt (because of the smaller number of persons affected) and harder (because those affected argue they are being unfairly singled out for higher taxes when the burden should be spread more evenly).

Such changes could include eliminating certain deductions such as those for part of state and local taxes, contributions to charity that are not in cash, reducing the losses from tax shelters that reduce the income the federal government can tax, and taxing certain benefits provided by employers ranging from free parking to generous health plans and personal legal services.

Better Enforcement

Many Americans believe that other Americans don't pay their fair share of taxes. Part of this feeling stems from features of the tax law that some people are in a better position to take advantage of than others. For example, those whose employers pay for health benefits are in a better position than those who must use after-tax money to pay for health insurance because their employers don't provide it. Those who can afford tax shelters do better than those who can't. These situations can only be addressed by changes in the tax law itself.

However, much of the concern is directed to those who pay less than the tax they owe because they get away with illegal conduct. Examples are not reporting income received in cash (e.g., waitress tips, some cab fares, money paid to plumbers and electricians in cash), keeping two sets of books in small business, and keeping income off the books by barter arrangements. Other concerns relate to questionable deductions, such as overvalued contributions to charity.

Some estimates of the revenue lost through tax evasion exceed $100 billion a year. However, this evasion won't be easy to stop. Much of it comes from activities that are already clearly illegal, such as drugs and prostitution.

39

Because society can't successfully prevent the activity, it is unlikely that government can monitor it well enough to collect tax on it.

Some forms of evasion could be prevented, however, by much closer IRS oversight of our personal financial transactions. One example is more complete reporting of tips that are charged to credit cards. Another is withholding of taxes from dividend and interest payments made by banks and other corporations. There is, of course, considerable public resistance to the added reporting and increased paperwork, as well as to the higher budgets IRS would need to use this information effectively.

Social Security Taxes, A Special Case

While payroll taxes for social security raise considerable revenue, they aren't considered a likely candidate for increase. All of the revenues from these taxes go to special funds used for paying social security benefits and certain health care costs for persons over 65. (As we will see in the next chapter, although these revenues are set aside, they do affect the overall budget deficit figure.) Laws already passed will cause these taxes to increase further over the next decade. Revenues from social security taxes will likely be sufficient to pay retirement benefits until well into the next century. Paying for health benefits is another matter, as discussed in the next chapter.

Summing Up

As this chapter shows, there is no shortage of ways for the federal government to close the deficit by raising taxes. The problem, of course, is that many Americans don't want to raise taxes. For those willing to consider this strategy, the table below gives an indication of how much money could be raised by the various choices.

Some tax law changes, such as rate increases, could be made immediately. Others, such as changing rules for corporate accounting, would probably be phased in over several years. To put these on a comparable basis, the table below shows how much various measures would raise in FY 1990. (Recall that the projected deficit that year is $296 billion.)

Table 4

Choices for Raising Taxes

THE TAX CHOICES	WHAT THEY RAISE ($ billion)
ENTIRELY NEW TAXES	
Sales or Value-Added Tax	
1% Rate	15
3% Rate	46
Consumption Tax	0-150
Revenue depends on tax design.	
Energy Tax (5%)	18
Personal Net Worth Tax (1% rate)	110
HIGHER RATES, INCREASING TAXES	
Surcharge on Individual Income	
(Per Percent)	5
Surcharge on Corporate Income	
(Per Percent)	1
Eliminating Indexing for Inflation	58
Sin Taxes (20 cents per pack of cigarettes	
increase and double tax on alcoholic	
beverages)	8
Gasoline (Per step of 10 cents per gallon)	9
REFORM PROPOSALS FOR CURRENT INCOME TAX	
Reduce Tax Shelters and Eliminate Oil	
Depletion and Drilling Allowance	15
Adopt Alternative Corporate Minimum Tax	10
Eliminate Deductibility of State and	
Local Taxes	51

Chapter Four

Cutting Federal Spending

Introduction

This chapter discusses current federal spending and the various choices for reducing it.

As it considers the deficit, the Congress is faced with many conflicting pressures. While many people want Congress to do something about the deficit and to cut federal spending, many people—often the same people—have specific programs they want the Congress to adopt or expand.

Where Federal Money Goes

The chart below shows the principal ways the federal government spends money.

Chart 11. Revenue Outlays—Fiscal Year 1990

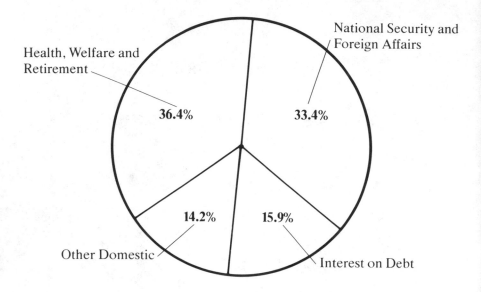

Source: Congressional Budget Office

There are arguments made that various parts of the budget should be exempt from budget cuts. But doing this substantially increases the cuts that would have to be made in the remaining programs. For example, suppose Congress wanted to reduce spending by $100 billion to try to close the deficit, allowing tax increases and savings in interest costs to do the rest of the job. What it would have to cut from FY 1990 spending is shown below in relation to exemptions from cuts.

Table 5

Percentage Cuts Needed to Save $100 Billion in FY 1990

Exempt These Items	and Cut This Much
Nothing	9.2%
Social Security (except medical)	12.0%
National Defense	15.1%
National Defense and Social Security	24.4%

44

Uncontrollable Interest Costs

Almost every week the Treasury Department goes to the public to borrow money to finance the current deficit and to repay the past borrowings that are due for repayment. There isn't much choice about this. If Treasury didn't do it, the government would literally run out of cash. Social security checks couldn't be mailed (or would bounce), and the government couldn't pay its employees and contractors. But when Treasury goes to market with debt, it is signing contracts to repay those who lend it money. Everybody agrees these contracts must be honored. If they weren't, no one would lend money to the federal government again.

Creditors are free to lend their money to the government or somebody else, so federal officials have no choice but to pay whatever the interest rates happen to be at the time they borrow. They can't set the interest rate because the marketplace does. The Treasury officials in charge of borrowing don't control how much they borrow either. That is determined by the difference between revenues and spending. Congress decides both of these. With no Treasury control over either the interest rates paid or the amount borrowed, interest on the federal debt is officially considered an "uncontrollable" federal expense.

Of course, interest costs can be controlled—but only through controlling the amount of debt being financed, which means dealing with the deficit. Thus, saving money on interest is not a direct means of reducing deficits, but rather a result of dealing with the deficit in other ways. For example, putting the nation's finances on a path that would cut $100 billion in FY 1990 from federal programs would also reduce the deficit enough to make interest costs about $35 billion lower in that year.

Trust Funds

About a third of the federal budget takes the form of trust funds. These funds contain money that is earmarked for particular uses and "held in trust," separate from other funds.

One example of this is the highway fund. The federal government imposes a tax on gasoline and diesel fuel designed to make the users of nationally important roads pay the costs of building and maintaining them. State governments manage similar funds for the state and local share of road work. Over long periods of time, these funds do not contribute to the deficit because their income and spending are pretty much equal. Cutting spending in a trust fund like the one for highways isn't likely to have much of a long-term impact on the deficit. If spending were cut, highway users would have a strong case that the taxes should be cut also. As a practical matter, the states would probably reimpose the same taxes in order to finance the

45

same level of spending. (This doesn't mean the federal government couldn't adopt a special extra tax on gasoline earmarked for cutting the deficit rather than building highways.)

Social Security Trust Funds

One critical issue in considering how to deal with the deficit is whether to consider social security trust funds at all. There are actually a number of trust funds involved, including ones for regular retirement and disability under social security, related retirement funds for railroad workers and coal miners affected by black lung disease, plus a hospital insurance fund.

If the federal government budgeted for these trust funds as it requires business to do and as state and local governments do, they would not be included in the total budget and no one would think of using surpluses in trust to offset a government operating budget. In practice, however, the government consolidates these accounts with the rest of the budget for purposes of both presentation and operation. If social security runs a surplus and the rest of the budget is in deficit, the overall deficit is reduced arithmetically by the amount of the social security surplus. And if the social security trust fund has a surplus, it lends the money to the rest of the government, which reduces the amount that has to be borrowed in the marketplace.

During the late 1970s, it became clear that the revenues of the social security system would be inadequate to cover its mounting outlays for pensions. Many controversial proposals to deal with the situation were put forward in the early 1980s. In 1983, the President and congressional leaders established a bipartisan task force, which made recommendations that were quickly adopted by the Congress. These tax increases and benefit reductions are generally believed to guarantee the system's solvency until well into the 21st century.

Because the social security problem is deemed to be solved, at least for a while, and because of fear of the political ramifications of reopening the subject, many political leaders don't want to consider budget cutting plans affecting social security. But others argue that social security is such a large part of the budget that any "balanced" plan for deficit reduction must involve it.

Since the time that the normal retirement age was set at 65, and at 62 for early retirement with reduced benefits, the longevity of Americans has increased by more than 10 years. As a result, many more persons live to retirement, and they live longer after they reach it. The most significant cost-saving measure in the social security retirement program would be to raise the retirement age to reflect this shift. However, it is generally believed to be unfair to have such changes affect those very near retirement. There-

46

fore, such a change in retirement age would probably be phased in so that workers within five years of retiring might not be affected at all; those within ten years of retirement might have their retirement date delayed by a matter of months; and the full delay would apply only to new workers. This means that the changes would have very little effect on federal spending over the next five years, where the concern over closing the deficit is concentrated.

Of much more immediate significance is what is done about cost of living increases in benefits (COLAs). Currently, benefits are increased every year to reflect increases in the cost of living in the preceding year. The result is to maintain the purchasing power of the benefits, but at considerable cost. It would be possible to cushion the impact of inflation partially, but not completely. For example, the COLA increase could be held to two-thirds of the cost of living increase. If inflation were 6%, benefits would only rise by 4%. Those who support such a move say social security recipients do not need full cost of living adjustments because they are sheltered from some cost increases (for example, they already own their homes and basic household possessions). Opponents argue that the change would be unfair and would push hundreds of thousands of retired people below the poverty line.

Another approach, sometimes advocated as part of a one-year freeze on federal spending, would be simply to skip a year of cost of living increases. This would save money in the year it was done and in every subsequent year because each year's increase is based on the amount of the benefit the prior year. Thus, having a lower benefit in one year compounds its effects over the lifetime of each retiree.

Social security is considered an "entitlement," that is, one earns the benefits upon retirement by contributing, along with the employer's matching contributions, during the period one works. Because rich and poor alike contribute, rich and poor alike get benefits. Millionaires get monthly checks just like other retirees. Moreover, the money to finance current benefits comes out of current taxes levied on everyone—in effect taxing the rich, poor, and middle class alike to pay benefits to the rich.

Some say this isn't right because the millionaires don't need the money. They want to reduce or eliminate benefits for those with high income from other sources. Those opposed to such changes reply that social security can't be preserved in the long run unless it remains a truly universal system.

Denying benefits to the rich could save substantial sums of money. How much would depend on such factors as the income levels defined as the cutoff point, the proportion of benefits denied, and the treatment of social security contributions made by those affected.

Health Care and Medicare

Medicare provides hospital insurance and out-of-hospital care for persons over age 65.

Like social security, the hospital insurance is handled by a trust fund financed by payroll taxes paid by employers and employees. Unlike social security, this trust fund is not solvent through the rest of this century. Experts differ on *when* trouble will occur but not on *whether* it will.

The reasons are understandable. As the over-65 population grows, the number of persons using the program has been growing more rapidly than has the number of active workers who pay for it. In addition, health care costs have been rising faster than prices generally, for several reasons. Advances in medical technology are making better care possible, but at a price. And for the past two decades, the system of health care payments has encouraged—indeed, virtually ensured—rapid inflation.

Congress has already taken some steps to control costs, including a new system for paying hospitals. But even if this helps control costs, it will not be enough. Thus, either there must be further cuts in the program, or some of the costs must be shifted to those who get the benefits, or payroll taxes must be raised, or some combination of these measures.

The out-of-hospital coverage (known as Part B) is not funded by payroll taxes. Instead, those who purchase the coverage pay about $15 a month for it and the federal budget covers the rest—$45 a month for each person enrolled. One way to cut federal spending would be to shift costs to those who get this coverage. They could be asked to pay higher premiums to reduce the general taxpayer subsidy or bear a larger share of the costs when they actually get treatment. Some people object to these ideas because of their impact on the elderly poor but wouldn't mind applying them to more affluent elderly persons.

The federal budget also covers other health care costs. Health benefits are provided to retired federal employees, to military personnel, to merchant seamen, to certain veterans and pregnant women, and a variety of other people. In addition, the federal government sponsors health research and subsidizes the education of doctors, nurses, and other health care specialists.

There is considerable interest in trying to hold down health care costs for everyone, not just the share that is paid from the federal budget. This is not easy. While many people think doctors make too much, they constitute only 9% of all the professionals working in health care. The rest of the health providers—nurses, orderlies, and others—are not generally regarded as overpaid. Furthermore, much of the cost of health care comes from goods sold in regular markets—food, fuel, beds and linen, cotton, and the like. Health care cost controls can also try to squeeze out inefficiency in the system, such as unnecessary tests and excessively long hospital stays. Some people believe that further moves in this direction could cut federal health care spending without damaging patient care; others have their doubts.

National Defense

Because defense constitutes about a third of the federal budget, it is difficult to talk about major reductions without considering defense. But this is hard for most Americans because they don't have a clear idea either of the distribution of defense costs or of the military capabilities of the United States and its adversaries.

The defense budget is currently divided by category as shown in the table below.

Table 6

Percentage Distribution of Defense Outlays, FY 1985

Category	Percent
Operations and Maintenance (including civilian personnel)	30
Purchase of Weapons	28
Military Personnel	27
Research and Development	11
Construction and Other	3

Another way of looking at the defense budget is by major mission. Items that cannot easily be attributed to particular missions, like research and training, account for much of the budget. Of the remainder, 16% is for "strategic" forces to deter and, if necessary, fight all-out nuclear war, while 84% is for what are called "general purposes" forces maintained for such duties as defending against a ground attack in Europe, invading Grenada, and maintaining a military presence throughout the world.

The defense budget is large—over $1,000 a year for every American. These resources buy considerable capacity: nearly 2.2 million men and women in uniform, services of about a million civilians in federal service and many more working for defense contractors, 17 Army divisions, 1,000 Minuteman strategic missiles, 96 attack submarines, 13 aircraft carriers and their supporting vessels, and more.

The cost of defense is fundamentally determined by three factors: (1) what, as a nation, we want to be able to accomplish with military force; (2) how effectively resources are used to accomplish these missions; and (3) the defense expenditures of actual or potential adversaries. Some people like to ask what is to be done and how it can be done most efficiently. Others focus on general decisions like the appropriate percentage of GNP for defense and annual rates of increase (or decrease) in inflation-adjusted defense spending.

Strategic Forces: The mission of our strategic forces is to deter a nuclear attack on the United States and to ensure that our country retains the post-attack capability to launch a devastating blow against the aggressor. To achieve this capability, we rely upon land-based missiles, submarine-based missiles, and bombers.

The U.S. bomber fleet is decades old, but still serviceable. However, technological advances in defenses against bomber attack suggest that much of the bomber fleet would no longer be able to reach heavily defended targets in the Soviet Union. Planned improvements in our airborne attack capacity would be new bombers—the B-1B and an advanced technology (Stealth) bomber—and cruise missiles to be launched by bombers from outside the effective range of most Russian air defenses. Current budget projections accommodate continued procurement of cruise missiles and B-1Bs, continuing development of the Stealth, and increased research and development on missile defense, including what has come to be known as the "Star Wars" program.

The level of spending needed for land-based strategic missiles is highly dependent upon whether our country wants a so-called "second- strike capability"—that is, the ability to absorb an initial attack and then retaliate effectively. Many consider this capacity to be essential. But today, the accuracy and number of Russian warheads are believed to be sufficient to knock out much of our land-based missile force, even in their hardened silos. Thus, to absorb a first strike while retaining an assured destruction capability, the United States would be almost completely dependent on missiles carried in submarines and bombers on alert. Many fear such heavy dependence on this capability because technological breakthroughs may some day make it possible to detect, shadow, and destroy submarines.

To have assured second-strike capability with land-based missiles, it is generally agreed that they must be mobile. Many different plans have been considered, such as putting missiles on rail cars or in a large system of silos, only a small percentage of which would be occupied at any one time. The President's current plan is to buy new (MX) missiles to replace existing (Minuteman) missiles and to deploy the MX in existing silos while seeking strategic arms limitation agreements with the Russians.

The budget projections also reflect a continued upgrading of submarine-based missile capabilities, including procurement of a new Trident submarine every year and replacement of current Trident missiles with new ones.

General Purpose Forces: The size and cost of other American forces is critically dependent upon two factors: (1) the magnitude and duration of the most difficult assumed mission and (2) the minimum capacity considered necessary during the most difficult mission to handle other situations with military force.

In military planning over the past several decades, the most demanding mission has been joining our NATO allies in the defense of Europe against ground attack from Warsaw Pact nations in a military action lasting a considerable period of time. Preparation for this contingency requires the stationing of Army and Air Force units in Europe and the pre-positioning of supplies and equipment for additional units to be transported from the United States. For such a conflict, it is assumed that a navy at least as large as the current one would be required to protect sea approaches to the battlefield. It is further assumed that the United States would wish to leave troops and ships deployed in the Pacific. It is generally agreed that any U.S. force with this capability would be able to handle other needs that might arise.

Given this mission, the assumption that Warsaw Pact countries will fight as a unit, and the current military posture of our European allies, the required general purpose force budget is expensive. Even with all of the defense spending in the baseline budget, it is not clear that NATO could stop the Warsaw Pact from a successful ground attack in Europe without employing nuclear weapons. (It is clear that considerably more spending than the baseline would be required to tackle the more ambitious mission of being able to fight a successful conventional war with the Soviets in the Middle East.)

The budget projections provide for expenditures consistent with the European mission—pre-positioned supplies in Europe for additional divisions, more air transport capacity, more sea transport capacity, purchase of 150 or more F-16s each year for the rest of the decade, over 700 new M-1 tanks a year, even more Bradley fighting vehicles (the successor to armored personnel carriers), new Navy fighters, continued ship procurement looking toward a 600-ship navy, plus research and development on new tactical weapons systems. Given the mission of a conventional war in Europe, the President and Congress have felt a sense of urgency about this pace of procurement. While most of our conventional weapons are considered the equal of Warsaw Pact weapons, not all of our troops have these weapons. Furthermore, fighting a conventional war in Europe assumes the use of National Guard units, many of which have weapons quite obsolete by our standards and, more important, by the Russians'.

Approaches to Defense Spending: Making a major reduction in the Defense Department budget by changing missions would require a decision that we would no longer strive for the capacity necessary to repel a Warsaw Pact ground attack in Europe by conventional means. This reduction could rest on one of two new policies: (1) that the U.S. would meet conventional aggression in Europe with nuclear weapons or (2) that the U.S. would make

51

an affordable commitment to European defense, but the decision of whether total NATO capacity was adequate or not would be left to those with the largest stake in the outcome— European governments.

Members of Congress and mainstream critics of defense spending have been very reluctant to question the key strategic and conventional missions driving the defense budget. Instead, they have concentrated on concepts of affordable defense spending and appropriate rates of growth in inflation-adjusted defense spending.

One approach to defense spending is historical. The implicit premise behind this approach is that historical patterns are an appropriate guide to current policy.

In real (inflation-adjusted) terms, the defense budget declined after the Vietnam War through the end of the 1970s. However, the largely favorable congressional response to President Reagan's proposals for substantial defense increases caused the defense budget to grow sharply (25% in real terms) from FY 1981 to FY 1984. Most of the increased spending has been in research, development, and procurement of weapons systems.

CBO's baseline budget assumes that real defense outlays will increase substantially. The administration's budget request is considerably higher than this. Holding the defense budget to zero real growth rather than the growth assumed in the CBO projections would save $7 billion in FY 1986, rising to $99 billion in FY 1990.

The history of defense spending can also be calculated by taking defense outlays as a percentage of GNP. During the Vietnam War, outlays for defense rose to nearly 9% of GNP, then fell gradually to about 5% of GNP in 1979 as GNP grew significantly faster than defense spending. It is currently about 6.5% and would rise to just below 8% if the administration's proposals were adopted. This would return it to about 1971 levels.

There is a widespread belief that all government agencies in general and the Defense Department in particular could be run more efficiently, getting more performance out of any given spending level. However, it is difficult to translate this belief into specific proposals. When this is done, as it was by the Grace Commission, the resulting savings estimates are widely criticized as unrealistic.

The operations and maintenance and military personnel components of the defense budget are basically a function of the size of the active forces. However, a major reduction of active forces in any of the three services would be inconsistent with a European conventional war mission. Reductions in the investment portion of the budget (construction, research and development, and procurement) are, in a sense, easier to make because the stated rationale can simply be the postponement of capabilities, not their total elimination. This "stretch-out" strategy, however, is not without cost.

Besides delaying the availability of weapons, it often increases their unit price by forcing inefficient production levels.

Assuming that partly finished projects are not canceled, cuts in procurement spending have little effect on outlays in the year for which the budget is being cut. Major weapons, particularly ships and aircraft, have long lead times, so most of the actual procurement spending in any year is the result of spending authorizations in prior years. Decisions to cut FY 1986 budget authority for procurement would be felt primarily in FY 1987-90.

Foreign Aid

The U.S. spends about $15 billion on foreign aid every year. About $10 billion of this is closely tied to the defense budget. This portion of the foreign aid budget provides military aid to certain allies and friends on whose forces we rely in the event of military action, as well as support to the economies of those countries. These outlays could be reduced, but only by accepting lower military capabilities in countries such as Korea. This in turn would mean relying more heavily on U.S. forces in the event we were to come to the defense of such nations if they were attacked.

About $5 billion of foreign aid spending in FY 1990 will be for economic aid not directly tied to defense needs. This includes U.S. contributions to multi-national development banks that make loans to less-developed countries, as well as direct economic aid. All or part of this assistance could be ended, at the expense both of improved living standards in less developed countries (which enhance their ability to purchase our exports) and of our ability to influence the decisions of their leaders.

The Safety Net

Most Americans believe that both compassion and good public policy require government to help the needy.

When government provides resources to poor persons, they are required to show that they are poor. Such programs are therefore known as "means-tested." The major federal means-tested programs (with expected FY 1990 spending) are:

> **Medicaid** ($33 billion, plus substantial state and local contributions): States administer health care assistance for all persons who receive cash welfare payments plus some other low-income persons. The program reimburses doctors, hospitals, and others who provide health care services to the poor.

> **Food Stamps** ($14 billion): The poor are given the opportunity to purchase food stamps, which substantially reduce their own costs for food.

Supplemental Security Income ($11 billion): Persons over 65, the aged, blind, and disabled are given cash assistance based upon a means test.

Assistance Payments ($10 billion plus substantial state and local contributions): This is what most people think of as welfare. The major program in this category, Aid to Families with Dependent Children, provides monthly payments to low-income single parents and, in some states, to couples where both parents are unemployed.

Child Nutrition ($5 billion): There is a range of programs designed to provide food to needy children, of which the school lunch program is the largest.

Veterans' Pensions ($4 billion): Certain needy veterans are entitled to pensions.

Other Means-Tested Programs ($7 billion): A variety of smaller programs are means-tested. Guaranteed college student loans are an example. The federal government also spends considerable sums on housing assistance for low-income individuals ($11-12 billion per year) but much of this spending even in 1990 will be driven by past commitments.

Other Programs

The major other programs of the federal government are shown with their 1990 spending levels below:

Table 7

Other Programs

Purpose	Cost ($ billion)
General Science, Space and Technology	10
Energy	4
Natural Resources and Environment	14
Agriculture	17
Commerce and Housing Credit	2
Transportation	33
Community and Regional Development	9
Education, Training, Employment, and Social Services	37
Health	48
Medical Insurance (Medicare)	112
Income Security (e.g., employee retirement and welfare)	145
Veterans' Benefits and Services	29
Administration of Justice	7
General Government	7
General Purpose Fiscal Assistance	8

Some of the largest costs are for retired federal employees— veterans, civil servants and military personnel, and special groups like railroad workers. It has been argued that benefits are too generous for these groups. However, what current retirees are paid is what they have been promised, so unless these commitments are breached, downward adjustments in benefits would primarily affect new retirees and have little impact on the deficit in 1990. However, many current retirees get annual cost of living increases. About $7 billion would be saved in FY 1990 if COLAs covered only two-thirds of annual inflation rather than all of it. Some of the more expensive and rapidly growing costs for veterans are unrelated to any disability they might have acquired while in service. Confining veterans' benefits (particularly free health care) to those whose health problems are service-connected would save about $10 billion.

Another approach is to examine the "safety net," the programs specifically for the poor discussed above. If persons who are physically able to work were excluded from benefits, whether or not they could find jobs, the savings would be about $25 billion, though there would be strong pressures on state and local government and private charities to help these people.

Yet another approach is to consider all of the money which the federal government provides to state and local governments. The argument for these programs is that there is a national interest in such things as pollution control and aid to the poor and that some state and local governments couldn't perform these functions without federal help. The argument against them is that if state and local officials want these programs, they should use their own taxes to pay for them. The total of state and local grants in 1990 is about $110 billion. However, cutting about $18 billion of this sum wouldn't result in savings to the federal government because these grants are financed by special revenues (e.g., the gas taxes for highway construction) that would logically revert to state and local governments along with the spending responsibility.

The remaining category can be described as the operating expenses of the federal government such as collecting taxes, running the Congress, maintaining national parks, the Coast Guard, and the like. Outlays for these types of activities will be about $50 billion in 1990. Budget projections assume that spending for them, primarily for federal wages and benefits, will grow to match inflation. Some sort of general freeze, including a long-term freeze on federal pay, could save about $5 billion, but it would be strongly resisted by the affected groups. A one-year freeze would save about $2 billion.

Summary

While the federal budget is large and complex, its magnitude is largely controlled by a few decisions.

Defense costs can be reduced by identifying objectives that could be altered to save money. Failing this, and lacking an easy way to identify and cut "waste," Congress affects the defense budget primarily through decisions on how fast to buy new weapons.

Social security can be excluded from consideration on principle, as some advocate. If not, the primary short-term choice is whether to provide recipients with full protection from inflation. For medicare and social security, there is also the question of whether affluent people should get benefits.

The remaining issues must either be dealt with individually, or some general logic—like the idea of a "freeze" on spending growth— must be applied to all of them.

Chapter Five

Changing Procedures
to Protect Against Deficits

Introduction

The Constitution provides that money cannot be spent by federal officials
except under an "appropriation" of funds made by Congress. Congress
makes funds available in appropriation bills, the legislation by which the
spending part of the budget is enacted. In carrying out these responsibilities,
Congress initially dealt directly with the heads of federal agencies and military commanders. One of the most vivid portrayals of the problems faced
by our forces encamped at Valley Forge during the Revolutionary War came
in a letter from George Washington that was actually a request to the Con-
tinental Congress for appropriations. As the government became larger,
however, this procedure became unwieldy. Accordingly, a law was passed
in the 1920s requiring the President to find out what the agencies wanted,
decide on what they should and shouldn't get, and provide the result to the
Congress as "the budget." The idea was that the President could relate the
needs of one agency to those of the others and offer an overall plan in light
of the money likely to be available from existing revenue sources plus any
new revenues he might care to recommend.

While this law required the President to examine the total picture in shap-
ing a budget, it did not impose a parallel responsibility on Congress. Congress was structured so that each piece of appropriations legislation was
considered by one committee. However, other committees had jurisdiction
over legislation which could affect spending by changing program characteristics (e.g., eligibility requirements for certain benefits). Furthermore,
tax policy and appropriations were handled in different committees, and the
two subjects were voted upon in separate pieces of legislation. Thus, it was
more than theoretically possible for Congress to be moving in one direction
on taxes and another on spending. This division of responsibility made it
possible for Members of Congress to vote for deficits without ever being
held accountable for doing so. That is, they could vote for tax cuts and

expenditure increases without ever voting directly on the deficit that would inevitably result.

Concern over this problem led Congress to establish its own budget procedure in the mid-1970s. Under this procedure, Congress takes a preliminary vote on the overall budget in the spring. This vote gives guidelines to the committees for their deliberations on taxes and spending. Then there is a "reconciliation" procedure in the summer through which Congress combines the work of the committees and votes again on general levels of taxes and spending. After this resolution is passed, there are various safeguards to make it difficult to pass any tax or spending bills inconsistent with it. Congress also established its own budget office, the Congressional Budget Office, as well as a budget committee in each House, each with a professional staff.

Many people believe that the new procedures have helped Congress make more rational decisions on spending and taxes. However, they haven't prevented unbalanced budgets, and they definitely didn't improve the performance of Congress in avoiding deficits, as shown below.

Table 8

Deficits Over Time ($ billion)

Years	Years without Deficit	Smallest Deficit	Largest Deficit
1961-65	0	1.4	7.1
1966-70	1	-3.2 (surplus)	25.2
1971-75	0	6.1	53.2
1976-80	0	40.2	73.8
1981-85	0	78.9	222.2

The Balanced Budget Amendment

Some Americans believe that the only solution for these escalating deficits is an amendment to the Constitution requiring the President and Congress to balance the budget every year. Forty-nine of our 50 states and most of our local governments have such requirements. The provision most commonly advocated would require a general balancing of the budget, with an exception permitted for a national emergency declared by a two-thirds majority of the Congress.

The opponents of the balanced budget amendment do include some groups that support higher federal spending for such objectives as education and federal employee pay and pensions. But other opponents have more general objections. Some of them believe that the federal budget should be used as a tool of economic management and therefore are not distressed when deficits arise in a recession, while others are supporters of balanced budgets who want decisions on budgetary balance to be made in Congress rather than written in concrete in the Constitution.

Item Veto

Another possible Constitutional amendment to fight deficits is the "item veto" which 43 governors have, but which the President does not. At present, the President has only the power to accept or reject bills as packages. If he uses his veto, Congress can override it with a two-thirds vote of both houses.

The veto is a powerful instrument for exercising presidential power; veto overrides by Congress are very uncommon. However, it is not particularly effective for dealing with an appropriations bill, which is typically passed shortly before the affected agencies need the authority to spend money provided by such bills. If the President vetoes the bill, Congress may not even try to override. Instead, it can simply send him another bill with comparable spending patterns. Meanwhile, there are strong pressures on the President to reach accommodation with the Congress so the agencies can continue operations. Moreover, the Congress is quite adept at combining in one measure provisions the President favors as well as the ones he dislikes, further decreasing his incentive to wield the veto.

With an item veto, the President could delete appropriations for particular programs, cut appropriations without eliminating them, and eliminate legal language that would require higher spending. With these changes, the bill could then be signed. Because the President could never add spending, just cut, many people who seek lower federal spending support the item veto. Opponents fear that it would give the President too much power over Congress. Instead, they think it is better for the President to be required to negotiate with congressional leaders over the spending cuts he wants.

The Power Not to Spend

The legislation establishing the congressional budget process took away a power the President used to have—the ability to decide not to spend funds that had already been appropriated. Now he can only do this subject to a variety of restrictions, including approval by Congress in certain circumstances.

Some think the law should be changed to give this "impoundment" power back to the President. Others fear that if he had this power he would use it primarily to make the cuts he recommended in the budget but which were not accepted by Congress, thereby thwarting the will of Congress and changing the balance of power between the President and Congress.

Changing the Process in Congress

The congressional budget process clearly has not worked as well as its sponsors hoped. Because it created new budget committees that affected the power of older appropriations and tax policy committees, its enactment involved considerable compromise that kept much of the power in those other committees. As a result, these committees do not always follow the guidelines developed in the budget process. Sometimes Congress as a whole has not followed them either, skipping one of the required steps, making appropriations much later than the schedule calls for or, in some cases, not making them at all but instead passing resolutions allowing agencies to operate on what amounts to a month-by-month basis.

As a result, it is still possible for Members of Congress to do the impossible—tell their constituents that they are simultaneously for specific measures to increase spending, for specific measures to cut taxes, and for reducing the overall deficit. Some people believe this will always be a problem unless one massive bill becomes the vehicle for passing major appropriations, tax law changes, and the budget plan. If this were done, Members of Congress could not vote to cut the deficit in the abstract. Instead, they would have to be specific about what taxes they wanted to raise or expenditures they wanted to cut. And they couldn't increase spending without recognizing the impact of their actions on the deficit.

The Power of Public Opinion

While all these procedural changes have possibilities, the most important single factor in our democratic country is what the American people think. More precisely, the important thing is what representatives of the people in Congress *think the people think*.

One of the problems Congress has is that it rarely hears from the average person. Instead, the people who write to Members usually have a particular interest. This means when it is examining spending, Congress tends to hear from people who want to spend money. When it considers spending for education it hears from parents, teachers, and professional advocates of education. When it considers spending for health care, it hears from doctors and other health care professionals. When it considers taxes, Congress hears from taxpayers who care about different provisions of the tax law but have in common their desire to avoid tax increases affecting them and to reduce their taxes if they can. Thus, if Congress lets spending outrun revenue and creates a big deficit, it is doing what the people seem to be telling it to do.

It is not surprising that few people have communicated forcefully with their representatives about the overall deficits. Our nation has little experience with peacetime deficits at current high levels. We have no experience with large deficits significantly financed by capital from other nations. Furthermore, the effects of deficits are difficult to understand.

Now that the recession of 1981-82 and the 1984 presidential election are behind us, the President and Congress may be in more of a mood to deal with the deficit, particularly as it becomes clear that economic recovery alone will not do the job. And now that it is evident that the recession was only part of the problem in key sectors of our economy, workers and their employers in the industries may also become more interested in the deficit.

Appendix

Next Steps

You have an important role to play in resolving the deficit crisis. Having just read this book, you know that the problem is serious and that solving it will demand the persistent application of political courage and discipline. That will require all of us, you included, to do our part. Before we explore what that part might be, let us first dispose of two myths that might deter you from getting involved.

Myth Number 1: I'm Not an Expert

If you have read this book, you know what the key decisions affecting the deficit are. And the fact is that the key judgments involved in this problem— as in most public problems—are matters of informed common sense about policies and priorities that don't have right or wrong answers.

Myth Number 2: There's Nothing I Can Do

The opposite is closer to the truth—there's almost nothing you can't do. Or, more importantly, there's nothing that can be done without you. The story of American politics is one of individuals gathering together to express their collective views for the benefit of the nation. As a practical matter, your elected representatives depend on your vote to stay in office. They will listen to your guidance if you offer it. On many issues, a handful of letters from constituents may determine how a Representative or Senator votes and whether he or she takes a firm stand. Here are just a few ideas about how you can contribute to reducing the federal deficit.

Learn More about the Problem
 • The list of added readings will enable you to supplement this handbook with detailed information in areas that specially interest you.

Support your Local Congressman and Senators

- Let your elected representatives know you realize that everyone will have to sacrifice to get deficits down and that you are willing to bear your share. Get others in the community to offer similar assurances. The attached outline of a letter to your representative should help you get started.
- Express an opinion on specific budget-cutting options. Help him or her by providing some idea of the hard choices you might favor. A budget balancing worksheet, printed below, should help you get a sense of your own deficit-reducing priorities.

Join with Others

- Organizations already exist that address this issue from a variety of political perspectives. See page 79 for the names and addresses of some prominent research and advocacy organizations.
- Create your own ad hoc study or action group to look for and promote local deficit cutting possibilities.
- Invite your elected officials to meet with your group to discuss the deficit issue.

Play DEBTBUSTERS

- DEBTBUSTERS is a group learning exercise designed by the Roosevelt Center to teach both the politics and the principles behind the deficit crisis. Participants play the roles of defense officials, welfare officials, tax-cutting members of Congress, and others with a stake in budget politics. You try to balance the fiscal 1990 budget without hurting your own piece of the budget pie. DEBTBUSTERS is being played by students and citizen groups throughout the country. For more information, see pages 65-75.
- Invite your Senators or Representatives to play DEBTBUSTERS.

DEBTBUSTING
AN EXERCISE IN DEFICIT REDUCTION

Following is a series of possible ways of either reducing federal spending or increasing taxes in fiscal year 1990. The options are based on those presented in DEBTBUSTERS, the Roosevelt Center's role-playing game. Budget choices are presented in four major categories:
- Defense and Foreign Affairs
- Health, Welfare, and Retirement Programs
- Other Domestic Programs
- Tax Policy

This exercise will help you see the difficult choices and trade-offs involved in resolving the deficit dilemma. Remember that each budget item has a vociferous lobby that will fight to ensure that the budget knife slices elsewhere. When you have finished you will have a better sense of how difficult balancing the budget will be, understand where the real savings are, and better appreciate the pressures your elected representatives face in attacking this problem.

CAN __YOU__ CLOSE THE DEFICIT GAP?

TAXES ────────────────────────▶

$10 Billion	$10 Billion	$10 Billion	$10 Billion	$10 Billion	$10 Billion	$10 Billion	$10 Billion	$10 Billion	$10 Billion	$10 Billion

DIRECTIONS

The "budget thermometer" above represents the spending-taxing gap now projected for fiscal year 1990. Each full block within the thermometer represents $10 billion. Your goal is to find $214 billion in specific deficit reductions choosing from among deficit-reducing options presented on the following pages. If you do this, interest payments on the national debt will be about $82 billion lower in 1990, closing the rest of the deficit gap.

For each deficit-reduction option you choose, shade in the number of $10 billion blocks that corresponds to the savings for that option. For instance, if you choose a $5 billion option, shade half a block; if you choose a $20 billion option, shade two blocks.

$4 Billion	$10 Billion	$10 Billion	$10 Billion	$10 Billion	$10 Billion	$10 Billion	$10 Billion	$10 Billion	$10 Billion	$10 Billion

For the three **spending** categories presented, start shading on the right-hand side of the thermometer and work your way left. For **tax** options, start at the left and work your way right. You might want to use a different color for each budget category. That way you will be able to see clearly where you made the biggest savings.

Remember that while deficits can hurt, so can spending cuts and taxes. You may find you are unable to increase taxes or cut spending enough to achieve a balanced budget. This is the situation your elected representatives face every year. You make the judgment.

When you are done, you have a picture of your own personal deficit-reduction priorities. If you can completely close the gap between taxing and spending, you have successfully balanced the fiscal 1990 budget!

GOOD LUCK!

DEFENSE AND FOREIGN AFFAIRS

I. LONG-RANGE STRATEGIC NUCLEAR ARMS

This category consists of the costs of forces necessary to launch a retaliatory nuclear attack on the Soviet Union and those forces, mostly in research now, that might make it possible for the U.S. to intercept and destroy Soviet strategic forces attempting to attack our country.

Choose any combination of strategic nuclear arms options:

- **Option 1**—Cancel B-1 Bomber and delay advanced bomber development.   SAVE $3 BILLION
- **Option 2**—Cancel MX Missile   SAVE $2 BILLION
- **Option 3**—Reduce strategic missile defense research to a slower pace.   SAVE $5 BILLION
- **Option 4**—Cancel Trident D-5 advanced submarine-based missile.   SAVE $3 BILLION

II. CONVENTIONALLY ARMED WEAPONS

Choose any combination of conventional arms options:

- **Option 5**—Eliminate some types of tactical fighters and helicopters.   SAVE $4 BILLION
- **Option 6**—Slow naval modernization.   SAVE $5 BILLION
- **Option 7**—Limit growth in military research and development.   SAVE $8 BILLION
- **Option 8**—Limit spending for support equipment such as trucks, office equipment, and training devices.   SAVE $9 BILLION
- **Option 9**—Cancel or curtail selected Army weapons that may be unnecessary or ineffective.   SAVE $1.2 BILLION

III. BENEFITS FOR RETIREES AND VETERANS

Military retirement policies are designed to encourage enlistment and keep our forces young. Pensions are now available after 20 years of service. The retirement policies for Defense Department civilians are less generous, but generally pay more and permit earlier retirement than those in the private sector.

Choose one or both benefits options:

- **Option 10**—Reduce cost-of-   SAVE $5 BILLION
  living increases in pensions, and
  cut pensions for those of
  working age.
- **Option 11**—Eliminate cost-of-   SAVE $4 BILLION
  living increases for high-income
  retirees, extend required military
  service for retirement to 25 years,
  and make civilians retire later.

IV. READINESS AND FORCE STRUCTURE

Choose one, two, or all three readiness options:

- **Option 12**—Slow rate of growth   SAVE $23 BILLION
  in operations and maintenance budget,
  which covers civilian employees, base
  maintenance, spare parts for weapons,
  fuel, training costs, and a host of
  other items necessary to support a
  fighting force.
- **Option 13**—Selective reductions: SAVE $10 BILLION
  close some military bases,
  reduce stockpiles.
- **Option 14**—Cut 250,000 active-   SAVE $21 BILLION
  duty troops from present level
  of 2.2 million; rely more on reserves.

V. FOREIGN AID

Two-thirds of the foreign aid budget provides military and economic aid to strategically important allies and friends. About a third of foreign aid spending in 1990 will be for economic aid not directly tied to defense needs.

Choose one foreign aid option **only:**

- **Option 15**—Cut current foreign aid   SAVE $9 BILLION
  levels in half.
- **Option 16**—Eliminate foreign aid   SAVE $16 BILLION
  almost completely.

HEALTH, WELFARE AND RETIREMENT

I. SOCIAL SECURITY

Social Security provides payments to persons who have retired after contributing to the system, to workers who become disabled, and to dependent survivors of contributors to the system.

Choose one Social Security option **only:**

- **Option 1**—Reduce cost-of-living   SAVE $30 BILLION
  adjustment to less than the rate
  of inflation.
- **Option 2**—Eliminate cost-of-   SAVE $11 BILLION
  living increases for persons with
  family incomes over $32,000 a year.
- **Option 3**—Combine Options 1 and 2.   SAVE $40 BILLION

II. MEDICARE

Medicare provides hospital insurance to persons over 65 and pays three-fourths of the cost of their insurance for out-of-hospital care. The Medicare fund is in trouble because existing revenues are proving inadequate to cover growing medical costs.

Choose one or both Medicare options:

- **Option 4**—Impose new cost controls   SAVE $15 BILLION
  and make elderly pay more for out-of-
  hospital care. New cost control
  measures would probably lead to some
  reduction in the quality of health care
  available to elderly Americans who
  depend on the program.
- **Option 5**—Make persons with annual   SAVE $10 BILLION
  family incomes over $32,000 pay more
  costs of their government health
  insurance.

III. ASSISTANCE TO THE POOR

This category covers the federal government's contribution to social welfare programs for the poor, including cash payments to the elderly poor, Medicaid for health care, food stamps, Aid to Families with Dependent Children, and housing assistance. Together, these programs make up the so-called social safety net for the poor.

Choose one assistance-to-the-poor option **only:**

- **Option 6**—Reduce free medical care, reduce housing subsidies, and tighten eligibility for assistance.   SAVE $10 BILLION
- **Option 7**—Freeze programs, offer no cost-of-living increases.   SAVE $14 BILLION
- **Option 8**—Provide welfare (housing, health, food, and other support) only to those physically incapable of working.   SAVE $25 BILLION
- **Option 9**—COMBINE Options 6 and 7.   SAVE $22 BILLION
- **Option 10**—COMBINE Options 6, 7, and 8.   SAVE $40 BILLION

OTHER DOMESTIC PROGRAMS

I. GRANTS TO STATES AND LOCALITIES

The federal government provides over $100 billion a year to state and local governments. Some of these grants pay for welfare and social assistance programs. Money for these programs is included in the Health, Welfare and Retirement category.

Choose one grants option **only:**

- **Option 1**—Eliminate aid for   SAVE $20 BILLION
  projects with primarily local impacts,
  such as local economic development
  and money to operate local bus
  and subway systems.
- **Option 2**—Eliminate most federal   SAVE $45 BILLION
  aid programs. This policy would
  take the federal government totally
  out of transit, pollution control,
  education, and streets and roads.

II. AGRICULTURE SUBSIDIES

Choose one agriculture option **only:**

- **Option 3**—Reduce price supports   SAVE $5 BILLION
  and eliminate subsidy for minor
  products such as peanuts,
  tobacco, and honey.
- **Option 4**—End subsidies for   SAVE $12 BILLION
  production of all agricultural
  products.

III. OTHER FEDERAL PROGRAMS

Choose any combination of options:

- **Option 5**—Charge admission and   SAVE $0.9 BILLION
user fees for national parks.
- **Option 6**—Require beneficiaries   SAVE $2.5 BILLION
of federally subsidized dams,
irrigation, hydroelectric and other
water projects to pay more.
- **Option 7**—Reduce scientific   SAVE $3 BILLION
research and the space program.
- **Option 8**—Eliminate federal support   SAVE $0.9 BILLION
for commercial energy development
including synthetic fuels.
- **Option 9**—Restrict federal law   SAVE $1 BILLION
enforcement to crimes closely
related to federal tasks such as
protecting federal officials,
customs, immigration control, and
prosecuting tax fraud.
- **Option 10**—Reduce federal health   SAVE $3.1 BILLION
research by half.
- **Option 11**—Eliminate subsidies   SAVE $0.9 BILLION
to Postal Service for charities,
nonprofit organizations, and operating
expenses.
- **Option 12**—Limit AMTRAK subsidies   SAVE $0.4 BILLION
to those absolutely necessary to ensure
service to low-volume communities.

TAX POLICY

I. NEW TAXES

Most federal revenue comes from the income tax. Many argue that income tax rates are too high and that tax evasion is too easy. Alternative tax proposals are, therefore, gaining popularity. They include:

- A **national sales tax** which would work basically like state sales taxes—every time you make a purchase you pay a few cents in tax for every dollar. The **value-added tax** (VAT) works much the same way, but the manufacturer, rather than the customer, pays it. A VAT or sales tax such as the one in the options list would exempt food, medicine, and housing from taxation.
- An **energy tax** would add to the cost of gasoline, other fuels, and electricity. While it would increase Americans' energy costs, it would also encourage conservation.
- Raising federal **excise taxes** on such products as cigarettes or alcohol could also produce increased revenues.

Sales tax or value-added tax (VAT)

Choose one VAT option **only:**

- **Option 1**—One-percent sales tax or VAT.   ADD $15 BILLION
- **Option 2**—Three-percent sales tax or VAT.   ADD $46 BILLION

Energy Tax

Choose one energy tax option **only:**

- **Option 3**—Five-percent energy tax.   ADD $18 BILLION
- **Option 4**—Ten-percent energy tax.   ADD $37 BILLION

Excise Taxes

- **Option 5**—Add 20-cent-per-pack cigarette tax and double taxes on beer, wine, and liquor.   ADD $8 BILLION

II. BROADENING THE INCOME TAX BASE AND CLOSING LOOPHOLES

Only about half of the money we earn is subject to the federal income tax. The other half escapes because it is not counted at all; it is counted on a reduced basis; or it is "wiped out" by deductions for charitable contributions, interest paid on consumer loans, state and local taxes, and other items. The federal government could raise billions of additional tax dollars without raising tax rates by enlarging the income base that is subject to taxes.

Choose any combination of options:

- **Option 6**—Eliminate oil depletion   ADD $15 BILLION
and drilling allowance and reduce
tax shelters.
- **Option 7**—Require all corporations   ADD $10 BILLION
to pay at least a minimum income tax.
- **Option 8**—Eliminate deductibility   ADD $51 BILLION
of state and local taxes.

III. GENERAL TAX INCREASES

Choose any combination of options:

- **Option 9**—Impose twenty-percent   ADD $21 BILLION
surtax on corporate profits. A
surtax is a "tax on a tax."
- **Option 10**—Repeal indexation of   ADD $58 BILLION
personal income tax. Indexation
prevents inflation from pushing
wage-earners into higher tax
brackets.

FOR MORE INFORMATION

The starting point for considering deficits is to review the budget sub-
mitted by the President and his recommendations for dealing with the deficits. The President's budget is published by the Government Printing Office
(Washington, D.C. 20402). The one published early in 1985 (Budget for
Fiscal Year 1986) will be the only one until early 1986. It comes in several
parts. *The Budget in Brief* ($2.50) is a summary of about 50 pages. *The
Budget* ($13.00) is a 450-page volume with more detail on taxes, spending,
and the President's plan plus all the tables you will probably want. The
volume entitled *Special Analyses* ($8.00) has specialized information such
as what it would cost to continue present policies; investment spending;
government employment; and grants to state and local governments. There
is also a massive *Appendix* which will be too detailed for many people to
find interesting.

Individual citizens can get free individual copies of the analyses which the
Congressional Budget Office (Second and D Streets, S.W., Washington,
D.C., 20515) does for Congress. The key books were published early in
1985. They are *Options for Reducing the Deficit* and *Baseline Estimates for
FY 1986-1990*. CBO does many good analyses of federal spending and
taxes; ask for a list when you get your basic volumes.

If you follow news magazines like *Newsweek, Time,* and *U.S. News and
World Report,* you will get an idea of what is going on in Congress and the
administration on taxes, spending, the deficit, and economic policy. For
more detailed coverage, your library may have publications like *Congressional Quarterly* and the *National Journal.*

A variety of groups have reports on the deficit. *Breaking the Deficit Deadlock: A Fair and Simple Plan to Balance the Budget* is a report of a bipartisan task force that is available from the Roosevelt Center for American
Policy Studies. The Brookings Institution has a publication on the deficit
called *Economic Choices,* Brooking also has a catalogue of publications that
may be of interest as does the American Enterprise Institute. The Heritage
Foundation has also published a report, *Slashing the Deficit.* (Addresses for
these organizations can be found at the end of this book.)

If you want to know more about deficits and their economic effects, government spending and budgeting, and tax policy, probably the best place to
start is with a current college textbook on public finance. Your nearest college or university bookstore should have one for sale. They can also be
found in many libraries. Try to get a recent edition.

SAMPLE LETTER TO MEMBER OF CONGRESS

(To get the full name and address of your Representative and/or Senator, you can call any library with a reference desk.)

Representative John Doe
(or Senator Jane Jones)
(Address)

Dear Representative Doe
(Dear Senator Jones)

I have been doing some reading about the impact of the federal deficit and want to share my opinions with you.

(Use this paragraph to give your feeling about the deficit—you think it's a very serious problem, you think people are overreacting to it, or whatever you think.)

(Use this paragraph to make your major point about what you want done—adopt the balanced budget amendment, tighten fiscal controls, cut defense spending, raise taxes or don't raise them, and so forth.)

(Use any additional paragraphs to elaborate on your views. For example, if you want certain forms of spending cuts, say as specifically as you can what you want cut and why. If there is certain spending you want increased or not cut, it can be helpful to specify it, too.)

Sincerely,

Your Name(s)

Don't forget to include your return address.

Most Members of Congress answer all their mail. In some offices, the Member will not see your letter until a staff member has read it and made recommendations as to what the Member should say in response.

If you decide to fill out the worksheet on the following page, you should consider sending it along also to give your representative more detailed insight into your thinking and recommendations.

WORKSHEET ON THE FEDERAL DEFICIT

This worksheet deals with the FY 1990 budget because policy changes often require several years for their effects to be fully realized and because most people believe that deficit reduction will be a gradual process leading to a target in a specific future year. The sheet assumes that the policies you endorse will be phased in starting with the budget for FY 1986, the year beginning in October of 1985. This phase-in will reduce deficits in years before 1990, making the debt and thus interest payments lower in that year by roughly the amount calculated on the worksheet.

This is the estimated FY 1990 deficit from
current policies: $296 billion

Pick the FY 1990 deficit you want: _____

Subtract: this is how much you want
the deficit cut   −   _____

Figure interest savings—how much you
will save in interest by steps to cut
the deficit as much as you want (26%
of your deficit cut number above as a
rough estimate).

                                                               _____

Subtract again: this is what you need
to get by cutting spending or increasing
taxes.   −   _____

YOUR PLAN

    RAISING TAXES. Amount of New
Revenue—Summarize below:

    CUTTING SPENDING. Amount of Spending
Cuts—Summarize below:

Total your proposed tax increases and spending cuts; this should equal what you wanted to cut, excluding the effects on interest. If it does, you have a plan to deal with the deficit. If it doesn't, you can change your target for cutting the deficit or revise your tax and spending plans.

ORGANIZATIONS

AMERICAN ENTERPRISE INSTITUTE
1150 17th Street, N.W.
Washington, DC 20036

202/862-5800

THE BROOKINGS INSTITUTION
1775 Massachusetts Avenue, N.W.
Washington, DC 20036

202/797-6000

CITIZENS AGAINST WASTE
1511 K Street, N.W.
Washington, DC 20005

1-800-USA-DEBT

COMMITTEE FOR A RESPONSIBLE
FEDERAL BUDGET
220 1/2 E Street, N.E.
Washington, DC 20002

202/547-4484

THE HERITAGE FOUNDATION
214 Massachusetts Avenue, N.E.
Washington, DC 20002

202/546-4400

PROPOSITION ONE
2100 M Street, N.W.
Suite 600
Washington, DC 20037

202/887-8101

ROOSEVELT CENTER FOR AMERICAN
POLICY STUDIES
316 Pennsylvania Avenue, S.E.
Suite 500
Washington, DC 20003

202/547-7227

Fiscal Child Abuse

"...And we expect you to pick up the tab!"

Where it comes from

Miscellaneous $142 billion 12.3%
Corporate income tax $107 billion 9.3%
Personal income tax $515 billion 44.7%
Social security taxes $389 billion 33.8%

Where it goes

Interest on debt $230 billion 15.9%
Other domestic $205 billion 14.2%
Health, welfare & retirement $526 billion 36.4%
National security & foreign affairs $482 billion 33.4%

CAN <u>YOU</u> BALANCE THE FEDERAL BUDGET? PLAY DEBTBUSTERS AND FIND OUT!

Test your political courage and negotiating skills as you devise your own proposal to reduce the federal deficit using actual figures from the Congressional Budget Office.

Play DEBTBUSTERS—a new and challenging federal budget balancing game. Assume the role of a political wheeler-dealer as you bargain, bully and lobby for your special interest.

No prior knowledge of the deficit or economics is required to play—only the desire to have fun and find out what the deficit deadlock is really about.

DEBTBUSTERS is for high-school and college students, associations and civic organizations, professionals, taxpayers and anyone who has ever wondered why the government can't live within its means.

Be a DEBTBUSTER! Send $14.95, along with the completed order form below, and receive all the materials you need for up to 24 people to play. Order today! Supplies are limited.